Basketball Guide, With Official Rules and Standard

Compiled by GLADYS E. PALMER, University of California Southern Branch
Revised by L. RAY BURNETT, M.D., Supt. City Recreation, Paterson, N. J.

BASKET BALL TECHNIQUE

FOULS

TECHNICAL FOULS (fouls not involving personal contact):

GUARDING FOULS—
1. Guarding over opponent.
2. Guarding around opponent.
3. Guarding with one or both hands over ball held by opponent.
4. Guarding with one or both hands touching ball held by opponent.
5. Guarding with both arms, when opponent is at a corner where two boundary walls meet.

FOULS WITH THE BALL:
1. Failure to throw ball within three seconds after it is caught.
2. Double dribble. (In dribble, bottom of ball must reach at least as high as knee.)
3. Double juggle. (In juggle, bottom of ball must go as high as top of head.)
4. Handing or rolling the ball to another player.
5. Throwing ball from kneeling or lying position.
6. Catching ball, on toss-up by Referee, before it has touched floor or has been touched by player other than those jumping.
7. More than one player of each team putting her hands on the ball when in tie with opponent.
8. Running with the ball.
9. Snatching or batting ball from opponent's hands.
10. Kicking or striking the ball.
11. Passing ball to another player while making a free throw for goal.

GENERAL FOULS—
1. Players jumping for ball must hold one hand behind the back and in contact with it.
2. Any persistent or intentional delay of the game.
3. Coaching from side lines by anyone officially connected with the teams.
4. Only the captains shall address officials
5. Failure of a substitute to report to scorer and be recognized by Referee before going on court.

PERSONAL FOULS (fouls involving personal contact):
1. Guarding with any part of the body touching opponent (properly termed "holding").
2. Holding, blocking, tripping, pushing, or constantly tagging an opponent.
3. Unnecessary roughness or unsportsmanlike conduct.
4. Pushing or holding an opponent who is in the act of throwing for the basket.

LINE VIOLATIONS:
1. Touching ground beyond field line division, or beyond second line if neutral space is used, with any part of body or clothing.
2. Touching or crossing free throw line before ball has touched basket or backboard.
3. Touching or entering free throw area, before ball tossed in free throw has touched basket or backboard.

PENALTIES
1. If overguarding opponent who is in the act of throwing basket—two free throws shall be awarded side fo...

A free throw shall be awarded side fouled ag...
NOTE—Five technical fouls disqualif...

Six fouls of any kind disqualif...

A free throw shall be awarded side fouled ag...
NOTE—Four personal fouls disqualif...
4 Two free throws shall be awarded.
1. An unguarded throw for opponent where ball is o...
2. Goal, if made, does not count, and whether ma... ball shall be put in play at center
3. If made by forward, goal shall not count. Ball is d... If made by guard, goal, if made, shall count. If n... free throw shall be awarded.

SCORING RULES
1. A goal made from the field shall count 2 points unless made by an overhead, two-hand toss, when it shall count 1 point.
2. A goal made from free throw shall count 1 point.
3. If ball, or basket, is interfered with while ball is on edge of, or within, basket—1 point.
4. A goal counts if whistle is blown while ball is in the air, except as specified in 5.
5. A goal thrown before whistle can be blown for a foul, made by team throwing it, shall not count.
6. A goal made from out of bounds or on unguarded throw after line foul shall not count.
7. In case of a tie, the game shall continue until either side has made two additional points (no change of baskets).
8. If the game is won by default, the score shall be 2 to 0.
9. If player of same team oversteps six-foot line (in free throw), the goal, if made, does not count.
10. If player from each side oversteps six-foot line (in free throw), the goal, if made, does not count.
11. If player taking free throw oversteps 15-foot line before ball has touched basket or backboard, goal, if made, shall not count.

THE BALL IS DEAD
1. After every field goal.
2. After a single free throw is made.
3. After double free throw on opposite sides, missed or made.
4. After double free throw for same side (if second is made)
5. At expiration of playing time.
6. When the ball goes out of bounds.
7. When the ball lodges in supports of basket.
8. After an illegal free throw.
9. When a foul or line violation is called.
10. When "tie ball" is declared.
11. When "time out" is declared.

RULES FOR "OUT OF BOUNDS" BALLS AND PLAYS
NOTE—A ball is out of bounds when it has completely crossed the boundary line.
1. A player may hold the ball five seconds out of bounds.
2. If ball is out of bounds, it is given to opponent of player last touching it.
3. If ball is played first in bounds by player who returned it from outside, it is given to her opponent at the same spot outside.
4. If player oversteps line when throwing in from out of bounds, the ball is given to her opponent at the same spot outside.
5. If ball is not thrown in at a point on a line drawn at right angles to boundary line at point where ball crossed it, an opponent shall have it.
6. If ball is batted out of bounds by one center, in jumping, it is given to an opponent outside.
7. If ball is batted out of bounds by both centers, in jumping, it shall be thrown up between them at a point three feet within the court, at right angles to point where ball crossed.
8. In case of doubt as to which side last touched out of bounds ball, it shall be tossed up between two opponents as described in 7.
9. If ball is out of bounds when "time" is called, play shall be resumed at the whistle just as if "time" had not been called.
10. All guarding must be done inside of the boundary line.

THE BALL IS THROWN UP BETWEEN PLAYERS
NOTE—The ball must be batted—not caught. The players jumping may not catch the ball until it has touched the floor or has been played by some other player than those jumping.
1. When ball is put in play at center. On center toss, if neither touches ball, toss again.
2. "Tie ball" (two opponents placing both hands on ball at same instant).
3. If ball is batted out of bounds by both jumping centers, the ball shall be thrown up between them at a point three feet within the court.
4. If ball is in bounds when "time out" is called, it shall be tossed up between players nearest the spot when "time out" was called.
5. If ball is held in tie between center and guard, or forward, the ball shall be tossed up between the center and a center opponent
6. In case of doubt as to who last touched the ball in "out of bounds," toss up (3 ft.) within court.
7. In case of doubt as to which player first had two hands on the ball, it shall be tossed up between the players in question.
8. If two players of different teams are over the division line at the same time, there shall be a toss-up between player who has the ball when the double violation is called and nearest opponent.

Gentlemen:

Enclosed please find $...

for which send me the articles listed below:

List Number	Quantity	Description of Article	Price

(See other side)

SPALDING'S ATHLETIC LIBRARY

Red Cover Series, 25c.   Blue Cover Series, 10c.   Green Cover Series, 10c.

No. 1R.	SPALDING'S OFFICIAL ATHLETIC ALMANAC. . . .	Price 25c.
No. 3R.	SPALDING'S OFFICIAL GOLF GUIDE.	Price 25c.
No. 6.	SPALDING'S OFFICIAL ICE HOCKEY GUIDE. . . .	Price 25c.
No. 55R.	SPALDING'S OFFICIAL SOCCER FOOT BALL GUIDE. .	Price 25c.
No. 57R.	SPALDING'S TENNIS ANNUAL.	Price 25c.
No. 59R.	SPALDING'S OFFICIAL BASE BALL RECORD. . . .	Price 25c.
No. 100R.	SPALDING'S OFFICIAL BASE BALL GUIDE.	Price 25c.
No. 200R.	SPALDING'S OFFICIAL FOOT BALL GUIDE.	Price 25c.
No. 700R.	SPALDING'S OFFICIAL BASKET BALL GUIDE. . . .	Price 25c.
No. 1C.	SPALDING'S OFFICIAL BASE BALL GUIDE (Canadian Edition) .	Price 25c.
No. 9.	SPALDING'S OFFICIAL INDOOR BASE BALL GUIDE.. .	Price 10c.
No. 7A.	SPALDING'S OFFICIAL WOMEN'S BASKET BALL GUIDE	Price 10c.
No. 12A.	SPALDING'S OFFICIAL ATHLETIC RULES (A. A. U.). .	Price 10c.

Group I.   Base Ball

"Blue Cover" Series, each number 10c.

No. 202. How to Play Base Ball
No. 350. How to Score   [ners")
No. 365. Base Ball for Boys ("Begin-
No.   9. Spalding's Official Indoor
          Base Ball Guide (including
          rules for Playground Ball)

"Red Cover" Series, each number 25c.

No. 59R. Official Base Ball Record
No. 100R. Official Base Ball Guide
No. 79R. How to Pitch
No. 80R. How to Bat
No. 81R. How to Umpire
No. 82R. Knotty Base Ball Problems
          ⎧ How to Organize a League
          ⎪ How to Organize a Club
No.   ⎨ How to Manage a Club
83R   ⎪ How to Train a Team
          ⎩ How to Captain a Team
No. 96R. How to Catch; How to Run
          Bases. New. In one volume.
No. 97R. How to Play the Infield and
          Outfield Positions.   En-
          tirely new. In one volume.
No. 98R. Ready Reckoner Percentages.
No. 1C.   Spalding's Official Base Ball
          Guide (Canadian Edition)

Group II.   Foot Ball

"Red Cover" Series, each number 25c.

No. 200R. Official Foot Ball Guide
No. 47R. How to Play Foot Ball
No. 55R. Official Soccer Guide
No. 39R. How to Play Soccer

Group III.   Tennis

"Red Cover" Series, each number 25c.

No. 57R. Spalding's Tennis Annual
No. 3C.   Spalding's Tennis Annual
          (Canadian Edition)
No. 2R.   Strokes and Science of Lawn
          Tennis
No. 76R. Tennis for Girls (Miss Ballin)
No. 84R. Tennis Errors and Remedies
No. 85R. Tennis for Girls (Mlle. Leng-
No. 99R. How to Play Tennis   [len)
No. 101R. The Outdoor Group or Com-
          munity Sports Club; How to Organize
          One. Includes directions for con-
          structing a tennis court
No. 102R. "The Kid"
No. 103R. The Club Player
No. 104R. The Expert

Group IV.   Golf

"Green Cover" Series, each number 10c.

No. 2P. How to Learn Golf

"Red Cover" Series, each number 25c.

No. 3R.   Spalding's Golf Guide, with
          revised rules
No. 4R.   How to Play Golf   [Leitch)
No. 63R. Golf for Girls (Miss Cecil

Group V.   · Basket Ball

"Blue Cover" Series, each number 10c.

No. 7A.   Spalding's Official Women's
          Basket Ball Guide
No. 193. How to Play Basket Ball

"Red Cover" Series, each number 25c.

No. 700R. Spalding's Official Basket
          Ball Guide   [for Women
No. 93R. How to Play Basket Ball.

Specially Bound Series of Athletic Handbooks

Any 25 cent book listed in Spalding's Athletic Library will be bound in
flexible or stiff covers for 50 cents each ; or any two 10 cent books in one
volume for 50 cents. One 25 cent book or two 10 cent books will be bound
in leather in one volume for 75 cents. Mention style binding preferred.

(Continued on the next page. Prices subject to change without notice.)

10-21

SPALDING'S ATHLETIC LIBRARY

Red Cover Series, 25c.　Blue Cover Series. 10c.　Green Cover Series. 10c.

Group VI. Skating and Winter Sports

"Blue Cover" Series, each number 10c.
No. 14　Curling
"Red Cover" Series, each number 25c.
No. 8R.　The Art of Skating
No. 20R.　How to Play Ice Hockey
No. 72R.　Figure Skating for Women
No. 90R.　Spalding's Official Ice Hockey Guide and Winter Sports Almanac (speed skating and ski records, snow shoeing and curling rules) [Edition]
No. 2C.　Ice Hockey Guide (Canadian

Group VII. Track and Field Athletics

"Blue Cover" Series, each number 10c.
No. 12A　Spalding's Official Athletic
No. 27　College Athletics [Rules AAU
No. 87　Athletic Primer
No. 156　Athletes' Guide
No. 182　All Around Athletics
No. 255　How to Run 100 Yards
No. 317　Marathon Running [petition
No. 342　Walking for Health and Com-
"Green Cover" Series, each number 10c.
No. 3P.　How to Become an Athlete
No. 4P.　How to Sprint
"Red Cover" Series, each number 25c.
No. 1R.　Spalding's Official Athletic Almanac [A.A.A A.
No. 45R.　Official Handbook Intercol.
No. 48R.　Distance and Cross Country Running
No. 70R.　How to Be a Weight Thrower
No. 77R.　A. E. F. Athletic Almanac and Inter-Allied Games.
No. 88R.　Official Handbook Can. AAU
No. 94R.　Olympic Games of 1920
No. 95R.　Official Handbook New England Intercollegiate A.A.

Group VIII. School Athletics

"Blue Cover" Series, each number 10c.
No. 246　Ath. Training for Schoolboys
"Red Cover" Series, each number 25c.
No. 61R.　School Tactics and Maze Running : Children's Games
No. 66R.　Calisthenic Drills and Fancy Marching and Physical Training for the School and Class Room
No. 74R.　Schoolyard Athletics

Group IX. Water Sports

"Blue Cover" Series, each number 10c.
No. 128　How to Row
No. 129　Water Polo
"Red Cover" Series, each number 25c.
No. 36R.　Speed Swimming
No. 37R.　How to Swim
No. 91R.　Intercollegiate Swimming Association Guide
No. 106R.　Science of Swimming
No. 107R.　Swimming for Women

Group X. Games for Women and Girls

"Blue Cover" Series, each number 10c.
No. 7A　Spalding's Official Women's Basket Ball Guide
"Red Cover" Series, each number 25c.
No. 38R.　Field Hockey
No. 41R.　Newcomb　[Leitch)
No. 63R.　Golf for Girls (Miss Cecil
No. 69R.　Girls and Athletics
No. 89R.　Learning Field Hockey
No. 93R.　How to Play Basket Ball, for Women

Group XI. Lawn and Field Games

"Blue Cover" Series, each number 10c.
No. 170　Push Ball
No. 201　How to Play Lacrosse
"Red Cover" Series, each number, 25c.
No. 6R.　Cricket, and How to Play It
No. 43R.　Archery, Roque, Croquet, English Croquet, Lawn Hockey, Tether Ball, Clock Golf, Golf-Croquet, Hand Tennis, Hand Polo, Wicket Polo, Badminton, Drawing Room Hockey, Garden Hockey, Basket Goal, Pin Ball, Cricket
No. 86R.　Quoits, Lawn Bowls, Horseshoe Pitching and "Boccie."
No. 101R.　The Outdoor Group or Community Sports Club: How to Organize One. Includes directions for constructing a tennis court.

Group XII. Miscellaneous

"Blue Cover" Series, each number 10c.
No. 13　American Game of Hand Ball
No. 364　Volley Ball Guide
"Red Cover" Series. each number 25c.
No. 49R.　How to Bowl
No. 105R.　Camps and Camping

Group XIII. Manly Sports

"Blue Cover" Series, each number 10c.
No. 282　Roller Skating Guide
"Red Cover" Series. each number 25c.
No. 11R.　Fencing Foil Work Illustra-
No. 19R.　Professional Wrestling [ted
No. 21R.　Jiu Jitsu
No. 25R.　Boxing
No. 30R.　The Art of Fencing
No. 65R.　How to Wrestle
No. 78R.　How to Punch the Bag

Group XIV. Calisthenics

"Red Cover" Series, each number 25c.
No. 10R.　Single Stick Drill
No. 16R.　Team Wand Drill
No. 22R.　Indian Clubs and Dumb Bells and Pulley Weights
No. 24R.　Dumb Bell Exercises
No. 73R.　Graded Calisthenics and Dumb Bell Drills

(Continued on next page. Prices subject to change without notice.)

10-21

SPALDING'S ATHLETIC LIBRARY

Red Cover Series, 25c.   Blue Cover Series, 10c.   Green Cover Series, 10c.

Group XV.   Gymnastics

"Blue Cover" Series, each number 10c.

No. 124. How to Become a Gymnast
No. 254. Barnjum Bar Bell Drill
No. 287. Fancy Dumb Bell and March-
ing Drills

"Red Cover" Series, each number 25c.

No. 14R. Trapeze, Long Horse and
Rope Exercises
No. 34R. Grading of Gym. Exercises
No. 40R. Indoor and Outdoor Gym-
nastic Games
No. 52R. Pyramid Building
No. 56R. Tumbling for Amateurs and
Ground Tumbling
No. 67R. Exercises on the Side Horse;
Exercises on Flying Rings
No. 68R. Horizontal Bar Exercises;
Exercises on Parallel Bars

Group XVI.   Home Exercising

"Blue Cover" Series, each number 10c.

No. 161. Ten Minutes' Exercise for
No. 185. Hints on Health   [Busy Men
No. 325. Twenty-Minute Exercises

"Red Cover" Series, each number 25c.

No. 7R. Physical Training Simplified
No. 9R. How to Live 100 Years
No. 23R. Get Well; Keep Well
No. 33R. Tensing Exercises
No. 51R. 285 Health Answers
No. 54R. Medicine Ball Exercises,
Indigestion Treated by Gymnastics,
Physical Education and Hygiene
No. 62R. The Care of the Body
No. 64R. Muscle Building; Health by
Muscular Gymnastics

Spalding Score Books, Competitors' Numbers, Etc.

BASE BALL SCORE BOOKS.

Made in three styles—Morse (Nos. 1, 3, 4, 5 and M); A. G. Spalding style
(Nos. 2 and S); John B. Foster style (No. F). The Spalding style has
diamond shaped spaces for scoring.

POCKET SIZE.

No. 1. Paper cover, Morse style, 7 games	Each	$0.20
No. 2. Board cover, Spalding style, 22 games	"	.50
No. 3. Board cover, Morse style, 46 games	"	1.00
No. F. Board cover, Foster (reporters') style, 79 games	"	1.50
No. M. Board cover, Morse style, 79 games	"	1.50
No. S. Board cover, Spalding style, 79 games	"	1.50

CLUB SIZE.

No. 4. Morse style, 8¾x10⅝ in., 30 games	Each	$2.00
No. 5. Morse style, 8⅜x10⅝ in., 79 games	"	3.00
Score Cards, 1 game	Dozen	.10

BASKET BALL SCORE BOOKS.

No. 10. Paper cover, 10 games	Each	$0.20
No. 11. Board cover, 25 games	"	.50
No. A. Collegiate, paper cover, 10 games	"	.20
No. B. Collegiate, board cover, 25 games	"	.50

TRACK AND FIELD, TENNIS AND GOLF SCORE CARDS.

No. TF. Olympic Score Card: for outdoor and indoor track and field athletic meets: used in A.A.U. championships	Each	$0.05
No. H. Tennis Score Card, endorsed by leading umpires: used in national championships, new and improved design; for five sets: in two colors	Dozen	.75
No. L. Golf Score Sheets: used in leading tournaments; size 22x28 in.; match play or medal play (specify which is wanted)	Each	.30

COMPETITORS' NUMBERS.

Used in A.A.U., intercollegiate and interscholastic championship events.
Made up in sets (1 to 50, 1 to 100, etc.).

Manila paper......Per number $0.02   Linen backed......Per number $0.12
Letters, A, B, C, D, etc., on manila paper, for relay races..Per letter .05

Any of the above mailed postpaid on receipt of price.

American Sports Publishing Company, 45 Rose St., New York

10-21

Questionnaire Blank

The questionnaire is inserted in each copy of the Basketball Guide for Women with the request that everyone playing the game will fill out these blanks and return them to the Committee. In this way everyone has an opportunity to send in his or her suggestions as to changes in the rules, and the Committee is kept posted on the progress of basketball all over the country and whether or not the rules are meeting the needs of different sections.

It is urgently requested, therefore, that everyone, after trying out the rules thoroughly during the winter, fill out the blanks and return them before March 15. Those received after this date cannot be used.

1. Have you found the last edition of the Official Rules satisfactory? ....

....

....

2. If not satisfactory, what suggestions would you make?.........

....

....

....

3. In the one division game—five on a side—do you think the center should or should not be allowed to shoot baskets? Why?......

....

....

....

Name ....

Address ....

Organization ....

Please return blanks to Miss Leslie Sawtelle, 105 South Huntington Avenue, Boston School of Physical Education, Boston, Mass.

Notice.—All questions on interpretations of rules should be addressed to George T. Hepbron, 45 Rose Street, New York City, rather than to the Questionnaire Committee.

SPALDING'S ATHLETIC LIBRARY
GROUP V, No. 7A

Official Basketball Guide For Women

CONTAINING THE

REVISED RULES

1921-22

EDITORIAL COMMITTEE

MISS ELIZABETH RICHARDS, Chairman
Smith College, Northampton, Mass.

L. RAYMOND BURNETT, M.D.
Supt. City Recreation, Paterson, N. J.

MISS HELEN FROST
Teachers' College, Columbia University, New York

AMERICAN SPORTS PUBLISHING COMPANY
45 ROSE STREET, NEW YORK

Committee on Women's Basketball

AMERICAN PHYSICAL EDUCATION ASSOCIATION

Miss Florence D. Alden, Chairman
Central School of Hygiene and Physical Education, New York.

Miss Henrietta R. Brown
University of Wisconsin, Madison.

Miss Margaret Burns
University of Chicago.

Miss Helen Frost
Teachers' College, Columbia University,
New York City.

Miss May Kissock
University of Minnesota, Minneapolis.

Miss Edna B. Manship
Wellesley College, Wellesley, Mass.

Miss Elizabeth Richards
Smith College, Northampton, Mass.

Miss Leslie Sawtelle
Boston School of Physical Education
Boston, Mass.

Miss Elizabeth R. Stoner
Mills College, California.

Miss Mary L. Woodford
University of California, Berkeley

Dr. L. Raymond Burnett
Supt. City Recreation, Paterson, N. J.

Dr. Harry Eaton Stewart
New Haven Normal School of
Gymnastics, New Haven, Conn.

George T. Hepbron, Secretary
45 Rose Street, New York City.

Editorial Committee
Miss Elizabeth Richards, Chairman
Miss Helen Frost
Dr. L. R. Burnett

Questionnaire Committee
Miss Leslie Sawtelle, Chairman
Dr. H. E. Stewart

Extension Committee

MISS HENRIETTA BROWN, Chairman
Chairman Middle West Sub-Committee.

MISS EDNA B. MANSHIP
Chairman Eastern Sub-Committee.

MISS ELIZABETH R. STONER
Chairman Far West Sub-Committee

MISS MARGARET BURNS

MISS MAY KISSOCK

MISS MARY L. WOODFORD

Middle West Advisory Committee

MISS MARJORIE BELL
University of Chicago.

MISS HELEN GATH
University of Missouri.

MISS KATHERINE BROWN
Indiana University.

MISS GERTRUDE HAWLEY
Northwestern University.

MISS HELEN BUNTING
University of Colorado.

MISS BEATRICE PEARSON
Milwaukee Downer College.

American Physical Education Association

DR. WILLIAM BURDICK, President

DR. J. H. McCURDY, Secretary

Committee on Women's Athletics

MISS ELIZABETH BURCHENAL, Chairman

MRS. SENDA BERENSON ABBOTT
MISS EUNICE ADEN
MISS FLORENCE D. ALDEN
MISS CONSTANCE APPLEBEE
MISS ELIZABETH BATES
DR. ANNA BROWN

DR. L. R. BURNETT
MISS MAUD CLEVELAND
MISS CATHARINE LEVERICH
DR. E. A. PETERSON
MISS FLORENCE SOMMERS
DR. H. E. STEWART

MISS WINIFRED E. TILDEN

Introduction

Very enthusiastic meetings for the discussion of basketball were held this year during the three conferences of the American Physical Education Association. Many valuable points were brought out from the free discussion, and greater unity of purpose and standards was evident everywhere.

The point that came up spontaneously and about which there was much similarity of feeling was that the two-hand overhead shot for the basket, near the basket, was so impossible to guard that the guard "might as well give the goal to the forward." A good deal of discussion arose, but no very adequate solution came out of it. The change that the Committee has formulated seems most nearly to satisfy the general feeling, but we are not at all sure it will remove the difficulty. We ask you all to try it open-mindedly and over an extended period of time. Then let us know the results and offer suggestions for a more adequate solution.

Often when we have asked for a tryout of some change, both instructors and students have been so sure "it would not work" that it scarcely could be called a tryout, and the play was used over such a short time that the players could not possibly have developed the necessary skill for making it successful. Please give this change the fairest kind of a chance.

The question of the inadequacy of most officials and coaches was discussed fully. As a result an effort is being made to establish a nation-wide board of officials. This will necessarily be a slow growth and needing the help of everyone interested in basketball.

All seemed to feel that the level of sportsmanship maintained in the game was dependent on the officials and coaches. H. S. Curtis in his book on play, quotes the manager of a large business concern as saying: "We never employ men from such and such a school. Their athletics teaches them to be crooked more effectively than their ethics department teaches them to be honest."

An ethics department cannot establish *habits* of honesty, for moral habits, as truly as habits of skill, are built up by doing by constant practice. The gymnasium and the playground are the places where that practice takes place, and it depends on the officials and coaches what habits will result. If they allow the hundred-and one little practices which no rules can possibly cover but which "no fellow would do," as Kipling has the Brushwood Boy say, the girls are getting fundamental training in evading the spirit of the law that will stay with them always. If you are a "real sport" you win by your own powers and skill—not by trickiness. Trickiness is the device of the weakling who can win no other way.

One of the startling weaknesses of our women in both business and social circles is their inability to face squarely the implications of failure. If a losing team is allowed to confuse its thinking by attributing their defeat to the cheating or roughness of the other team or to the unfairness of the referee, they are building habits of evading moral issues that will cripple them in all their dealings in life. They will swell that large mass of people who go through life attributing all their failures to graft on the part of their successful opponents, or to pull, money, friends at court, etc. The only way to improve in basketball—or in life—is squarely to assume the full responsibility for not making good ; to analyze our weaknesses and to build upon them for greater strength next time.

The forming of these habits and many others is in the hands of the officials and coaches. It seems therefore eminently worth while to see that the standard of officiating is as high as one can possibly make it.

FLORENCE D. ALDEN,
Chairman Basketball Committee.

Editorial Comment

BY MISS ELIZABETH RICHARDS, CHAIRMAN EDITORIAL COMMITTEE.

The Rules this year present few changes. The most important one is that included in Rule 9, Section 1, which changes the value of a goal from the field to *one* point instead of *two, when the goal is made by a two-hand overhead throw.* This change was made in an attempt to meet the demand for easier guarding rules. The Committee felt that to alter the guarding rules themselves would lead to rough play and personal fouls. The overhead shot is the most difficult one to guard, and, by minimizing the value of a basket made by this shot, the Committee hopes to better balance offensive and defensive play.

Two other less important changes are those in Rule 5, Section 4, permitting a player to re-enter the game, and Rule 15, Subdivision C, which disqualifies for a sum total of six fouls, personal and technical combined. There are other minor changes and suggestions which involve no real change of ruling.

The Committee again clamors for suggestions from the country at large. Do you like the new six-team ruling? Do you feel that the ruling on the overhead shot meets the request for easier guarding rules, or do we need to go one step further? Is there any rule which you feel should be eliminated? Think over these points, and send your opinions and suggestions, along with the questionnaire in the front of the Rule Book. It is through your suggestions and criticisms that the Committee can be made to feel the real needs of the game, and can more intelligently work toward making the A.P.E.A. Rules the best possible rules for the greatest number of people.

REFEREES AND UMPIRES.

BY MISS LESLIE SAWTELLE.

It is felt by many that the rules do not need revising so much as that they need more careful interpretation and study by officials, more rigid enforcement during games. To make playing more uniform, will referees, umpires and coaches pay more particular attention to the following:

1. Line violations are often caused by pushing by an opponent. Try to see this and call the pushing rather than the line violation.

2. Distinguish between guarding one who *has* the ball, and in scrimmage where neither has it and both have equal right.

3. A "charging" foul should often be called on the forward, instead of "blocking" on the guard.

4. The *umpire* is particularly requested to make her job as responsible a one as the referee's. There are some things that the referee cannot see well and which the umpire should particularly be on the watch for, *i.e.,* (1) hand coming from behind the back, (2) blocking and holding, (3) pushing, etc., and other things done by players who *have not* the ball.

    Umpires should not feel that they are criticizing the referee when they call fouls, but should make it their duty to see everything that the referee either does not or can not see. This will give the referee a feeling of much greater security and support.

5. Get the habit of counting, either aloud or to oneself, to prevent the foul of holding the ball, as soon as player gets ball in hand.

6. Look to see that player out of bounds keeps *both* feet out.

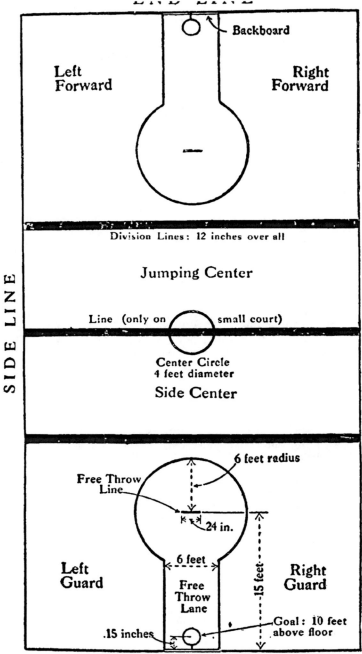

DIAGRAM OF BASKETBALL FIELD, SHOWING PERMANENT LINES.
Minimum court, 20ft. by 50ft., use two divisions; regulation size court, 35ft. by 70ft., use three divisions; maximum court, 50ft. by 90ft., use three divisions.

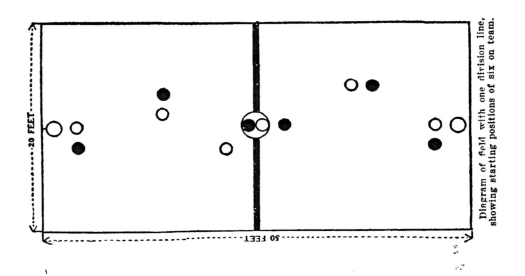

Diagram of field with one division line,
showing starting positions of six on team.

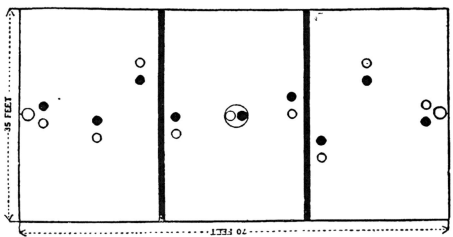

Diagram of field with two division lines,
showing starting positions of nine on team.

PLATE I—WRONG GUARDING; NOT IN VERTICAL PLANE,

Women's Official Basketball Rules

Adopted June, 1899, at Springfield. Mass.; Revised by Executive Committee of the Basketball Rules Committee, October 23, 24, 1905, at New York City. Revised September, 1908; Revised September, 1910; Revised September, 1911; Revised September, 1912; Revised September, 1913; Revised September, 1914; Revised March, 1916; ·Revised Sept., 1917; Revised May, 1918; Revised May, 1919; Revised September, 1920; Revised September, 1921.

THE GAME.

The Game of Basketball for Women is played by two teams of five, six or nine players each. The size of the floor used for playing determines whether the smaller or larger number of players is used. The ball is passed from one player to another, the purpose of each team being to get the ball into its own basket, and, at the same time, to prevent the other team from securing possession of the ball or scoring. A goal made from the field counts two points, unless made by an overhead shot; a goal made from a free trial, or from the field by an overhead shot, counts one point.

EQUIPMENT.
RULE 1.

SECTION 1. The *Playing Court* shall be a rect- **Court.** angular surface. free from obstructions. The maximum dimensions shall be 90 feet in length by 50 feet in width; the minimum, 50 feet in length by 20 feet in width. The regulation size shall be 70 feet in length by 35 feet in width.

NOTE—By mutual agreement of the captains, Section 1 and the distance of the boundaries from obstructions named in Sec. 2, may be changed.

SEC. 2. The court shall be marked by well **Boundary Lines.** defined lines, which shall be not less than 2 inches in width, and which shall be at every point at least 3 feet from any fixed obstruction. The lines on

PLATE II—CORRECT GUARDING.

the short sides of the court shall be termed the **RULE 1.**
End Lines; those on the long sides, the *Side Lines.*

SEC. 3.   The *Center Circle* shall have a radius of Center Circle.
2 feet, and it shall be marked in the center of the
court.   (See diagram on page 6.)

SEC. 4.   The *Field* shall be divided into three Division Lines.
equal parts by field lines, parallel to the end lines.

SEC. 5.   The *Field Lines* shall be 12 inches wide. Width of
Each may consist of two parallel lines forming a Field Lines.
neutral space 12 inches wide over all.

SEC. 6.   When, however, the length of playing Small Playing
floor is 50 feet or less, the field shall be divided Floor.
into two equal parts by one field line, parallel to the
end boundary lines, provided the total playing space
does not exceed 1,600 square feet.

SEC. 7.   The *Free Throw Lines* shall be marks, Free Throw Lines.
24 inches in length and 1 inch in width, the middle
points of which shall be on the straight line connecting the middle points of the end lines.   They
shall be marked in the court parallel to and at a distance of 15 feet from the inner edges of the end
lines.

SEC. 8.   The *Free Throw Lanes* shall be spaces Free Throw Lanes.
marked in the court by lines perpendicular to the
end lines at a distance of 3 feet on either side from
the middle points of the end lines.   These perpendicular lines shall be terminated and the lines
further marked by arcs of circles having a 6-foot
radius with centers at the middle points of the
free throw lines.   (See diagram on page 6.)

RULE 2.

SECTION 1.   *Backboards* must be provided, the Backboards.
dimensions of which shall be 6 feet horizontally
and 4 feet vertically.   The backboards shall be of
plate glass or wood or of any other material which
is permanently flat and rigid.

PLATE III—GUARDING AROUND; WRONG HORIZONTAL GUARDING.

SEC. 2. The backboards shall be located in a position at each end at right angles to the floor. Their centers shall lie in the perpendiculars erected at the middle point of the end lines.

RULE 2.
Position of Backboards.

SEC. 3. The backboards shall be protected from spectators to a distance of at least 3 feet.

Spectators 3 feet from Backboards.

RULE 3.

SECTION 1. The *Baskets* shall be nets of cord or other material, suspended from metal rings 18 inches in inside diameters. The nets shall be so constructed or tied as to check the ball momentarily as it passes through the basket.

Baskets.

SEC. 2. The *Rings* shall be rigidly attached to the backboards at a point 1 foot from the bottom and 3 feet from either side, supported by a horizontal arm, which if extended would pass through the center of the rings. The rings shall be placed in such a position that they shall lie in a horizontal plane 10 feet above the floor and so that the nearest point of the inside edge shall be 6 inches from the playing surface of the backboard.

Position of Rings for Basket.

RULE 4.

SECTION 1. The *Ball* shall be round; it shall be made of a rubber bladder covered with a leather case; it shall be not less than 30 nor more than 32 inches in circumference, and it shall weigh not less than 20 nor more than 23 ounces.

Ball—Material, Size and Weight.

SEC. 2. The *Home Team* shall provide a new ball, or two good used balls, satisfactory to the Referee. If used balls are provided, the visiting team shall choose the one with which the game shall be played, and they shall have it as their practice ball. If a new ball is provided, neither team shall use it in practice.

Choice of Ball.

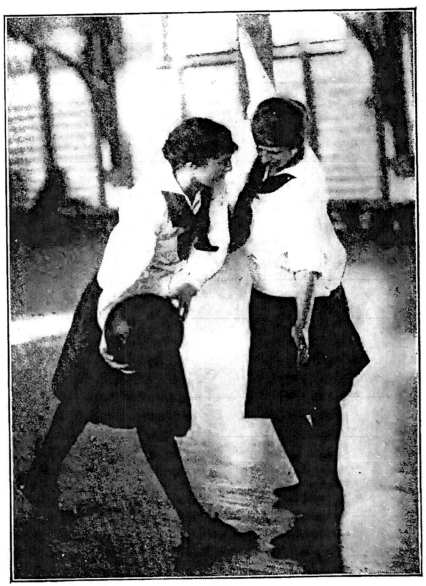

PLATE IV—CORRECT HORIZONTAL GUARDING.

RULE 5.

PLAYERS AND SUBSTITUTES.

SECTION 1.   Teams shall number not less than *Teams.* five nor more than nine players, one of whom shall be captain.

SEC. 2.   The captain shall be the representative *Captain—Duties* of the team and shall direct and control its play. *and Powers.* The captain shall, before the game starts, furnish **Scorers** with names and positions of players and substitutes.   The captain only may address any official on matters of interpretation or to obtain essential information when necessary, if it is done in a courteous manner.

If for any reason the captain does not play, the captain shall appoint a substitute to act during the time the regular captain is not playing.

SEC. 3.   Those playing the position of forward, *Positions in* of guard, or of center, must stay in their respective *Divisions.* sections except during "time out," or between halves.

When, however, the field is divided into two sec- *Centers May* tions, and a team consists of five players, the cen- *Not Throw for* ters *only* may run from one part of the field into the *Basket.* other.   When a team consists of six players, the centers must stay on that side of the line on which they began playing, and there shall be no crossing of this line.   Centers or guards in neither the one-division nor the two-division field may throw for basket.

NOTE—If one-division line is used with five players, centers should wear conspicuous emblems to mark them from the other players.

SEC. 4.   A substitute before going upon the court *Substitutes—* shall report to the **Scorer**, giving name and posi- *When and How* tion.   A substitute shall not enter the court *Put In.* until play has been suspended and shall not participate in the game until officially recognized by the **Referee**.   *A player who has left the game for* **New Ruling.**

PLATE V—WRONG PLAYING AT TOSS UP.

reason other than disqualification, may re-enter it RULE 5.
once only. As soon as the ball is dead, for any reason, or whenever play can be suspended without disadvantage, the **Referee** shall allow the substitute to enter the game.

SEC. 5. A player may not leave the playing court Players without permission of the **Referee** or the **Umpire** Leaving Court. until time is called at the end of the half.

RULE 6.
OFFICIALS AND DUTIES OF OFFICIALS.

SECTION 1. The officials shall be a **Referee**, an Officials. **Umpire**, two **Timekeepers**, two **Scorers**, and two **Linesmen**.

NOTE—It cannot be too strongly emphasized that the **Referee** *and* **Umpire** *of a given game should not be connected in any way with either of the organizations represented, and that they should be thoroughly competent and impartial. Upon agreement of the captains with the* **Referee** *and* **Umpire**, *the linesmen may be omitted. The* **Referee** *and* **Umpire** *should wear uniforms distinct from those of either team. The officials have no authority to agree to changes in the rules, except those mentioned in Rule 1, Section 1 (Note), and Rule 8, Section 1.*

SEC. 2. The *Visiting Team* shall choose the Choice of **Referee**, but shall notify the home team before Referees. the day of the game. Failure to send such notification shall forfeit the team's right to choose the **Referee**.

SEC. 3. The **Referee** shall: Duties of
1. Put the ball in play. Referees.
2. Decide *a.* when the ball is in play;
  b. when the ball is dead;
  c. when the ball is held in tie;
  d. to whom the ball belongs;
  e. when a goal has been made.
3. Call fouls and administer all penalties.
4. Recognize substitutes.

PLATE VI—UNDERHAND PASS FOLLOWING A PIVOT.
Guard about to pass to Center; pivot has been made on the right foot.

5. Call "time out" when necessary. RULE 6
6. Decide who had ball before "time out" was called.
7. Announce each goal as made, indicating with raised fingers the point value of the goal.
8. Publicly announce the score at the end of each half.

The final announcement of the score terminates the **Referee's** official connection with the game.

SEC. 4. The **Referee** shall notify any player who Player has made four personal fouls or five technical fouls, Removed. or a total of six personal and technical fouls combined, or a disqualifying foul, that the player has thus become automatically disqualified.

SEC. 5. The **Referee** shall have power to call Referee Decides fouls for unsportsmanlike conduct on the part of Points Not any player, *or to discontinue the game for persistent* Covered in Rules. *unsportsmanlike conduct on the part of spectators.* **New Ruling.** The **Referee** shall also make decisions on any points not specifically covered in the rules.

SEC. 6. Neither the **Referee** nor the **Umpire** Not to Question shall have authority to set aside or question deci- Each Other's sions made by the other within the limits of their Decisions. respective duties, as outlined in these rules.

If the **Referee** and the **Umpire** make approximately simultaneous decisions on the same play, and the decisions involve different penalties against the same team, the one drawing attention to the graver of the two shall take precedence.

SEC. 7. The **Referee** and the **Umpire** shall have Time and Place power to make decisions for violations of rules com- for Designations. mitted either within or outside the boundary lines; also at any moment from the beginning of play to the call of time at the end of the game. This includes the periods when the game may be momentarily stopped for any reason. Fouls may be called on any number of players at the same time.

PLATE VII—CHEST PASS FOLLOWING A DODGE.
Side Center has dodged with a step right.

SEC. 8. The official calling the foul shall designate the offender. A personal foul shall be indicated by the official raising a hand over head.

RULE 6. Designation of Fouls.

SEC. 9. The **Referee** shall call "time out" in case of injury to players. The **Umpire** may stop the game by blowing a whistle, in case of injury to a player which the **Referee** does not see, but "time out" is taken only upon order of the **Referee**.

Injury to a Player.

SEC. 10. The home team shall choose the **Umpire**, but shall notify the visiting team of such selection before the day of the game. Failure to send such notification forfeits the team's right to choose the **Umpire**. The **Umpire** shall call fouls committed by any player, but *shall pay particular attention to the players in the back field away from the ball, and to the free throw lines during a free throw*. The **Umpire** may, when requested by the **Referee**, assist in out of bounds decisions and shall co-operate in enforcing the rule against coaching.

Choice and Duties of Umpire.

SEC. 11. The **Scorers** shall, working together, keep one record book, in which shall be recorded the goals made and the fouls committed. They shall distinguish in the record between personal and technical fouls. They shall notify the **Referee** immediately when three personal fouls or four technical fouls, or a total of five personal and technical fouls combined, have been called on a player, in order that the **Referee** may warn that player. They shall again notify the **Referee** when the fourth personal foul or the fifth technical foul, or a total of six personal and technical fouls combined, has been called on a player, so that the **Referee** may disqualify such player.

Duties of Scorers.

The record kept by the **Scorekeepers** shall constitute the official score of the game. In case of any disagreement concerning the scoring, the scorers shall at once refer the disputed point to the **Referee**, who shall decide the matter. If the

Official Score.

Dispute Between Scorers.

PLATE VIII—OVERARM PASS.

Guard has the ball: she has turned away from her opponent, carrying the ball back and assuring its safe delivery.

Scorers fail to notify the **Referee** at once, the RULE 6. latter shall decide in favor of the smaller score, unless other knowledge permits a decision without reference to the **Scorers.** The **Scorers** shall be provided with a horn or whistle with which to signal the **Referee.**

NOTE—The sounding of the **Scorers'** *horn or whistle does not stop the game. It is suggested that the* **Scorers** *differentiate between personal fouls, P, and technical fouls, T.* (See model score card on page 46.)

SEC. 12. The **Timekeepers** shall note when the Duties of game starts, shall deduct time consumed by stop- Timekeepers. pages during the game on order of the **Referee,** and shall indicate with gong or whistle the expiration of the actual playing time in each half. Upon the sounding of the **Timekeepers'** signal, play shall cease instantly, except that if the ball is in the air on a try-for-goal when the **Timekeepers'** signal is sounded, play shall continue until the ball has entered or missed the basket. The **Timekeepers'** signal terminates actual playing time in each half.

NOTE—It is suggested that the **Timekeepers** *use one stopwatch placed on a table before them or on a wall hook, so that both may see it.*

SEC. 13. The officials shall blow a whistle when- Whistle— ever necessary to make a decision and shall an- When Blown. nounce decisions of fouls, score, etc., so that players, **Scorers** and spectators may hear it.

NOTE—It is desirable for all officials of a game to have different sounding whistles.

SEC. 14. The **Linesmen** shall be appointed, one Linesmen. from each side, by the management of the home team, and shall be subject to the approval of the **Referee.**

SEC. 15. The **Linesmen** shall stand at the ends Position of of the division lines. Their particular places shall Linesmen. be assigned them by the **Referee.**

PLATE IX—DRIBBLE FOLLOWING A PIVOT ON THE RIGHT FOOT AND A STEP
FORWARD LEFT.

Forward has the ball; on receiving it she was covered closely and is using the
combination pivot and dribble to get free and shoot.

SEC. 16. The **Linesmen** shall be judges of violations made by stepping beyond the field lines or touching the ground beyond the field lines with any part of the body or clothing. The **Linesmen** shall call such violations.

RULE 6.
Linesmen
Judge and Call
Line Violations.

RULE 7.

PLAYING TERMS.

SECTION 1. A *Goal* is made when the ball enters the basket from above, the impetus having been legally given by any player within bounds.

Goal.

NOTE—If the ball. passes through the basket from below and then enters from above, a goal is not made.

SEC. 2. *Out of Bounds*—A player with the ball is out of bounds when any part of the body touches the floor outside of the boundary line, except as provided for in Sec. 8, Note.

Player Out
of Bounds.

The ball is out of bounds when any part of it touches the floor outside the boundary line, or any object outside the boundary line, or when it is touched by a player who is out of bounds. The ball is caused to go out of bounds by the last player touched by it before it crosses the line.

Ball Out
of Bounds.

Who Causes
Ball to Go
Out of Bounds.

SEC. 3. *"Time Out"* is declared whenever the game can be legally stopped without disadvantage to either side; i. e., at time of a center toss or a tie ball.

"Time Out."

SEC. 4. *Tie Ball* is declared when two opposing players of opposing teams place both hands on the ball at the same time.

Tie Ball.

SEC. 5. A *Foul* is a violation of a rule for which a free throw is given.

Foul.

SEC. 6. The *Ball is Dead* and play shall cease until the ball again is put in play, in a manner indicated by the **Referee:**

Dead Ball.

a. When the goal is made. (Center toss.)

b. When the ball goes out of bounds,

PLATE XI—FORWARD DODGING PAST GUARD
TO RECOVER JUGGLED BALL AND
SHOOT FOR BASKET.

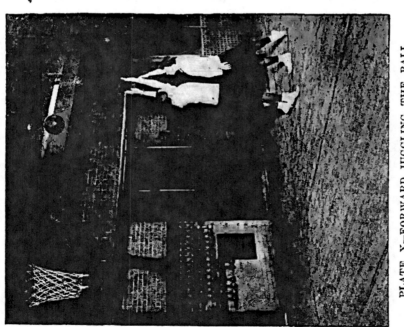

PLATE X—FORWARD JUGGLING THE BALL
OVER GUARD.

c. When tie ball is declared.

d. When "time out" is declared.

e. When a foul or line violation is called.

f. After each of the two free throws following a double foul. (Center toss after second.)

g. At expiration of playing time.

h. When the ball lodges in the supports of the basket. (Toss up, at a point near the basket, between player who threw the ball and an opponent selected by referee.)

i. After the first of two free throws following two fouls on the same team.

j. After an illegal free throw. (Center toss.)

NOTE—If on a try-for-goal the ball is in the air when the signal is sounded, as in Sec. d, e, f and g, the ball shall not be dead until it has entered or missed the basket. If, however, a foul is called on the team throwing for goal, the ball shall be dead at the time the foul is committed and the goal if made shall not count.

SEC. 7. A *Dribble* is a play in which a player, after giving impetus to the ball by bouncing it, touches it again before it has been touched by another player. Dribble.

A *Juggle* is a play in which a player, after giving impetus to the ball by throwing or batting it into the air, touches it again before it has been touched by another player. Juggle.

A *Bounce* shall be understood to mean a play in which the player, after giving impetus to the ball by bouncing it, does not touch it again before it is touched by another player. Bounce.

NOTE—Successive tries for goal shall not be considered dribbling or juggling; a player is permitted to shoot for the basket at the termination of a dribble or a juggle.

PLATE XII—CHEST SHOT FROM FREE THROW LINE.

Sec. 8. A player shall be considered as *Running* **RULE 7.**
with the Ball if, while having the ball constantly in Running with
hand, the player advances in any direction. the Ball.

*NOTE—A player who is standing still when re-
ceiving the ball may step with one foot in any
direction in making a pass or in starting a dribble
or juggle, but the remaining foot must be kept in
position until the ball has left the hands. A player
who is standing still when receiving the ball, may,
in throwing for goal, step or stride with one foot
in any direction, and then may jump from one or
both feet; but the ball must leave the hands before
one or both feet again touch the floor. Due allowance is to be made for catching the ball while running, provided the player throws it at once or stops
as soon as possible. If, however, at the end of the
run the player has one foot over the boundary line,
no action shall be taken if that foot is immediately
withdrawn; but if the foot that is inside the field is
carried outside so that both feet are outside, the ball
shall be given to an opponent out of bounds.*

*A player with the ball may turn around, pro-
vided one foot be kept in place, and shall not be
considered as running with the ball; neither shall a
player pushed by one of the opposing side be considered as running with the ball.*

Sec. 9. *Blocking* is impeding the progress of Blocking.
an opponent who *has not* the ball.

*NOTE—This includes holding extended arms in
front of opponent who has not the ball.*

Sec. 10. A *Free Throw* for goal is the privilege Free Throw.
given a team to throw for goal from a position
directly behind the free throw line.

Sec. 11. A *Double Foul* is made by both teams Double Foul.
having fouls called against them simultaneously.

Sec. 12. *Delaying the Game* is unnecessarily in- Delaying
terfering with the progress of the game by a player. the Game.

PLATE XIII—CROSS BODY SHOT.

Sec. 13. *Own Goal* is the basket for which a **RULE 7.** team is throwing. Own Goal.

Sec. 14. *Extra Period* is the extension of playing Extra Period. time necessary to break a tie score.

Sec. 15. *Personal Foul* is holding, blocking, trip- Personal Foul. ping, pushing, charging, or committing any other form of unnecessary roughness.

Sec. 16. *Technical Foul* is any foul not involv- Technical Foul. ing personal contact.

Sec. 17. *Disqualifying Foul* is rough play for Disqualifying which a player is removed from the game. Foul.

Sec. 18. Guarding with one or both hands over Overguarding the ball or touching the ball legally held by an Ball. opponent shall be termed *Overguarding*.

Sec. 19. Overguarding one's opponent consists Overguarding of: Opponent.

  a. Guarding with one or both hands or arms or body not in the vertical plane. (Plates I and II.)

  b. Guarding round opponent's person. (Plates III and IV.)

  c. Guarding with any part of body touching opponent.

  d. Guarding with both arms, when opponent is at a corner where two boundary walls meet.

Sec. 20. Guarding with any part of the body Holding touching an opponent, or constantly tagging an op- Opponent. ponent who has not the ball, shall be termed *holding*.

NOTE—Any interference with a player jumping for a tossed up ball shall be construed as holding.

Sec. 21. *Holding the Ball* is retaining possession Holding Ball. more than three seconds in the court, without hav-

PLATE XIV—OUT OF BOUNDS.

Side Center using overhand pass to Forward who is signaling for the ball to be sent toward the basket. Note that the out-of-bounds player is back from the boundary line and therefore the opposing Side Center does not do useless guarding at the line.

ing thrown, dribbled or juggled the ball; or more **RULE 7.**
than five seconds out of bounds.

SEC. 22. Touching the ground in bounds beyond Line Violation.
the field division line, with any part of the body or
clothing, shall constitute a *Line Violation.*

RULE 8.
PLAYING REGULATIONS.

SECTION 1. The game shall be started by the Length of Game.
Referee, who shall toss the ball up between two
players of opposite teams, as provided in Sec. 8,
9 and 11 of this rule. The game shall consist of
two halves of 15 minutes each, with an intermis- Intermission.
sion of 10 minutes between the halves. This is
the time of actual play. These times may be
changed by mutual agreement of the captains and
Referee. When a foul is committed simultaneously
with, or just previous to the sounding of the **Timekeepers'** signal, time shall be allowed for the free
throw.

*NOTE—In games between secondary schools or
in playgrounds, etc., where the players are not
mature, it is recommended that the game consist
of eight-minute quarters, with two-minute intermissions between the first and second quarters and
between the third and fourth quarters, and a ten-
minute intermission between the second and third
quarters. It is further recommended that for children fifteen years and under, the quarters be six
minutes, with three minutes rest between quarters
and ten minutes rest between halves. During the
two-minute and three-minute intermissions, the
players shall not leave the floor, receive coaching or
exchange goals. At the beginning of each quarter
the ball shall be put in play at the center.*

SEC. 2. Both teams must be ready to play within Winning
ten minutes after the game is called by the **Referee.** by Default.
If, at the expiration of this time, only one team is

PLATE XV—POOR OUT-OF-BOUNDS PLAY. Her opponent in bounds is right in guarding her.

The Side Center has space to step back, but stands at the line to deliver the ball.

ready, that team wins by default. If neither team has completed its number, the first team to do so may not claim the game by default until an additional five minutes shall have been allowed the other team to complete its number.

Captains shall be notified three minutes before the termination of the intermission. If either team is not on the floor ready for play within one minute after the **Referee** calls play, either at the beginning of the second half or after "time out" has been taken for any reason, the ball shall be put in play in the same manner as if both teams were on the floor ready to play.

Captains Notified at End of Intermission.

SEC. 3. The visiting team shall have choice of baskets in the first half. In intramural games, the captains shall toss for choice of baskets; for the second half, the teams shall change baskets.

Choice of Baskets.

SEC. 4. *A.* When catching a ball, two hands are necessary to secure it; but if caught, it may be legally retained in one hand or thrown with one hand.

Two Hands Necessary to Secure Ball.

B. A foul shall be called on a player who puts a hand on the ball after an opponent has secured it.

C. **Referee** shall decide which player first gained possession of the ball and shall award the ball to that player.

NOTE—A foul shall not be called on a player, who, in attempting to catch a ball, puts one hand on the ball after the opponent has secured it, provided the player immediately takes the hand away.

D. Not more than one player of each team shall touch the ball at the time it is being disputed with an opponent. Violation of this rule is a foul.

No More than One Player of Each Team on Ball.

NOTE—It is not a foul for two players on the same team to put their hands on the ball when it is not disputed by an opponent, provided one player immediately takes her hands away.

RULE 8.
Ball to be
Thrown within
Three Seconds.

SEC. 5. When a ball has been caught it must be thrown within three seconds. If the player has fallen down, the three seconds are counted from the time when all the body weight is again on the feet. Foul for delay may be applied if the player does not get up as soon as possible.

Ball Thrown, etc.,
in Any Direction.

SEC. 6. The ball may be thrown, dribbled, batted, bounced or juggled in any direction. The ball may be bounced or dribbled once only, with one or both hands, and the bottom of the ball must reach at least as high as the knee in bouncing. The ball may be juggled once only, and the bottom of the ball must go as high as the top of the head during the juggle. A dribble shall not be used combined with a juggle.

NOTE 1—For successive tries at basket, see Rule 7, Sec. 7, Note.

NOTE 2—While making the one bounce or one juggle, a player may take any number of steps, provided the steps are made between the time the ball leaves the hands and the moment it is again caught.

SEC. 7. No player may hand or roll the ball to another player. The ball must be thrown or bounced to another player or thrown for the basket. The player, when throwing the ball, must be standing on one or both feet or jumping in the air.

When Ball is
Tossed up
in Center.

SEC. 8. *A.* The ball shall be put in play in the center circle:

    a. At the beginning of each half.

    b. After a goal has been made.

    c. After an illegal free throw has been made.

    d. After the last free throw following a double foul.

    e. At the beginning of the additional playing period necessary in a tie score game.

B. When the ball is put in play in the center, each center player shall stand with both feet within own half of the center circle, with one hand behind **RULE 8.** the back and in contact with it; the hand shall remain in this position until the ball has been tapped by one or both players. The other players may take any position upon the court they may desire, provided they do not interfere in any way with the Referee or center players.

SEC. 9. When the **Referee** puts the ball in play *Referee Tosses* in the center, it shall be tossed upward in a *Up Ball Between* plane at right angles to the side lines between the *Centers.* center players, to a height greater than either of them can jump, so that it will drop between them. Both players must jump for the ball at center and elsewhere. The **Referee** shall blow a whistle when the ball reaches its highest point, after which it *Centers Must* must be tapped by either one or both of the center *Tap Ball First.* players. *The players shall not leave the floor until* **New Ruling.** *the whistle has sounded.* If the ball touches the floor without being tapped by one of the jumpers, the **Referee** shall put it in play again in the same place. If the ball is batted out of bounds by either of the players, the regular out of bounds rules shall apply (see Rule 10).

SEC. 10. When the **Referee** tosses the ball up *When Ball is* between two players elsewhere than in the center, *Tossed Up* the players shall assume the same position in rela- *Elsewhere than* tion to each other as when jumping in the center. *in Center.*

SEC. 11. Whenever the ball is tossed up by the **Referee** between two players, whether in the center or elsewhere, the ball must be batted, not caught. Neither of the players jumping may catch the ball until it has touched the floor or has been played by some other player than those jumping. This does not prevent the player from batting the ball more than once.

SEC. 12. The game shall terminate by the sounding of the **Timekeepers'** signal indicating the end of the game.

RULE 9.

SCORING.

Value of Goals.
New Ruling.

SECTION 1.   A goal from the field shall count two (2) points, *except for a two-hand overhead shot* when the basket, if made, shall score but one (1) point.

NOTE—The new ruling above is intended to discriminate against the two-hand overhead shot because it cannot be guarded under the present girls' rules. A two-hand overhead shot is one in which the ball is delivered from a point over or behind the head. See Plate II for position "over the head"; picture the ball back five or six inches to illustrate "behind the head." Any shot from the chest or shoulder cannot fall in this classification, nor can any one-hand shot be so classified.

Score of
Forfeited Game.

SEC. 2.   The score of a forfeited game or a game won by default shall be 2—0.

SEC. 3.   A game shall be decided by the scoring of the most points in the playing time.

Requires Two
Points to Win in
Case of Tie.

SEC. 4.   If at the expiration of playing time the score is a tie, the ball shall be put in play in the center and the game continue without exchange of baskets until either team has made two additional points.   The goals may be made either from the field of play or the foul line.   The team first scoring two points wins.

NOTE—In case of a tie and both teams make the second points simultaneously through both teams scoring on double fouls, the game shall continue as provided for in Rule 13, Sec. 3a.

SEC. 5.   Any team refusing to play after receiving instruction to do so from the **Referee** shall forfeit the game.

RULE 10.

OUT OF BOUNDS.

SECTION 1. If at any time during the game the ball goes out of bounds it shall be so declared by the **Referee** and put in play again by an opponent of the player who caused it to go out of bounds, said opponent to stand out of bounds at right angles to the spot where the ball left the court. The ball shall then be thrown or bounced to another player within the court. Unnecessary delay in recovering ball from out of bounds is considered delaying the game.

How Ball is Put in Play when Out of Bounds.

NOTE—When the space out of bounds is limited for any reason, no player of either team, except the player who has the ball outside, shall be nearer than three feet to the boundary line. It is wise to have a fine line drawn in the court three feet inside the boundary lines.

SEC. 2. If the **Referee** is unable to determine which player touched the ball last before it went out of bounds, the ball shall be put in play at a spot about three feet within the court, at right angles to the point where the ball crossed the boundary line, the **Referee** selecting two opponents and tossing the ball up between them as for tie ball.

How Ball is Put in Play if Referee is in Doubt as to Who Caused it to Go Out of Bounds.

RULE 11.

TIME OUT.

SECTION 1. *"Time Out"* shall be taken only when ordered by the **Referee**. "Time out" shall be ordered for not more than five minutes at the request of a captain or for injuries to players.

"Time Out" on Order of Referee Only.

NOTE—If the **Referee** *orders "time out" at the request of a captain more than three times during a game for one team, that team shall be penalized for delaying the game and a technical foul shall be charged against the captain.*

RULE 11.

After "Time Out" Ball is Tossed Up Unless it is in Possession of Player or Foul is Called.

SEC. 2. When the **Referee** declares "time out" or orders time to be taken out, the ball, on resumption of play, shall be tossed up between the two players of opposing teams nearest to it, at the spot where it was when play ceased. If, however, the ball is in the possession of a player when time is called, it shall be returned to that player when play is resumed. If the ball is out of bounds when time is called. it shall be put in play as for out of bounds (see Rule 10); if a foul is called, play shall be resumed with the free throw for goal.

SEC. 3. Time shall be taken out for a double foul.

RULE 12.

TIE BALL.

SECTION 1. When *Tie Ball* is called, the **Referee** shall take possession of the ball. The two players who have the ball shall assume positions similar to the centers at the start of the game, but in an imaginary circle at the spot where the ball was held. The ball shall then be put in play as at the center.

NOTE—If. however, the ball is held in tie between the center and forward or guard (over the field line), the ball shall be tossed up between the center and a center opponent indicated by the **Referee.**

RULE 13.

FREE THROW.

Procedure when Foul is Called.

SECTION 1. When a foul has been called, the **Referee** shall immediately secure possession of the ball and place it upon the free throw line of the team entitled to the throw. The throw for goal shall be made within ten seconds after the ball has been placed upon the line.

SEC. 2. If the goal is made, the ball shall be put in play at the center.

SEC. 3. If the goal is missed, the ball continues in play except:

a. That in case of a double foul, the ball is dead after the first throw and shall be put in play at the center after the second throw.

b. When two or more free throws are awarded a team, the ball is dead after each free throw except the last one. If the goal is missed after the last throw, the ball continues in play.

RULE 14.
VIOLATIONS AND PENALTIES.

A Player Shall Not—

SECTION 1. While making a free throw, touch or cross the free throw line, until the ball has touched the basket or backboard.

PENALTY— (SECTION 1.)
Goal if made does not count, and, whether made or missed, the ball shall be put in play at the center.

SEC. 2. Cause the ball to go out of bounds.

SEC. 3. Carry the ball into the court from out of bounds.

SEC. 4. Touch the ball after putting it in play from out of bounds, until it has been touched by another player.

SEC. 5. Interfere illegally with player who is returning the ball into court from out of bounds.

SEC. 6. Hold the ball more than five seconds out of bounds before putting it in play.

PENALTY— (SECTIONS 2, 3, 4, 5, 6.)
Ball goes to an opponent out of bounds.

RULE 14. SEC. 7. Touch ground beyond field line divi-
Over the Line sion or beyond second line if neutral space is
Violation. used with any part of body or clothing. (This
does not debar a player from leaning over the
field line to pick up or receive the ball.)

PENALTY—   (SECTION 7.)

a. If the violation is made by the team which is
in possession of the ball, the ball shall be
given to the opponent nearest the spot where
the ball was at the time the violation was
called. This opponent shall have an unguarded
throw to another player, but may not shoot
for the basket until the ball has been touched
by some other player.

b. If the violation is made by the team not in
possession of the ball, the player who has the
ball retains it and is allowed an unguarded
throw, but may not shoot for basket until it
has been touched by some other player.

c. If a double violation is made (two members
of different teams over the line at once), there
shall be a toss up between the player who
has the ball when the double violation is called
and the nearest opponent.

SEC. 8. Enter the free throw lane or touch free
throw lines, or attempt to disconcert the player with
the ball while a free throw for goal is being made,
until the ball has touched the basket or backboard.
If players contend for positions along the free
throw lanes, the **Referee** shall arrange the players
so that the desirable positions are evenly divided.

PENALTY—   (SECTION 8.)

a. For violation by a player of the team throwing
for goal, the goal if made shall not count, and,
whether made or missed, the ball shall be put
in play at the center.

b. For violation by a player of the opposite team,
the goal if made shall count, and, if missed,
another free throw shall be allowed.

c. For double violation by members of opposite
teams, the goal if made, does not count, and if
missed, the ball shall be considered in play.

Sec. 9. Throw for basket from out of bounds. **RULE 14.**

Sec. 10. Throw for basket while playing the position of guard or center.

Sec. 11. Throw for basket when ball is dead.

Sec. 12. Throw for basket on an unguarded throw following a line foul.

PENALTY— (Section 9, 10, 11, 12.)
> Goal if made does not count; if not made, ball shall be considered in play.

RULE 15.

FOULS AND PENALTIES.

A. Technical Foul.

A Player Shall Not—

Section 1. Run with the ball, snatch or bat the ball from the hands of an opposing player, kick it, strike it with the fists, roll it, bounce, dribble or juggle it more than once, or hand it to another player. **List of Technical Fouls.**

Sec. 2. Delay the game by touching the ball after it has been awarded to an opponent, or by leaving the court, by removing hand from behind back on the jump ball before the ball is tapped, or otherwise violating the jumping rules when the **Referee** tosses the ball up between two players, by not getting up quickly after falling down, by consuming more than 10 seconds in making a free throw, or in any other manner unnecessarily delay the game.

Sec. 3. Hold the ball in play constantly in one or both hands more than three seconds.

NOTE—If the player has fallen down, the three seconds are counted from the time when all the body weight is again on the feet.

RULE 15.   SEC. 4.   Pass the ball to another player while making a free throw for goal.   (An honest attempt to cage the ball must be made.)

SEC. 5.   Make a second bounce, dribble or juggle without first having passed the ball to another player.

SEC. 6.   Go on the court as a substitute before reporting to **Scorer** and being officially recognized by the **Referee.**

SEC. 7.   Overguard opponent who is not throwing for the basket.

PENALTY--   (SECTIONS 1, 2, 3, 4, 5, 6, 7.)
Free trial for goal given to opponents.

SEC. 8.   Interfere with the ball or basket while the ball is on the edge of or within the basket.

PENALTY—   (SECTION 8.)
One point awarded to team trying for goal.

SEC. 9.   Overguard an opponent who is in the act of throwing for the basket.

PENALTY—   (SECTION 9.)
Two free trials for goal.

SEC. 10.   There shall be no coaching from the side lines during the progress of the game by any one officially connected with either team, nor shall any such person go on the court during the progress of the game except with the permission of the **Referee** or **Umpire.**

PENALTY—   (SECTION 10.)
Free throw fer goal. A technical foul charged against the captain of the offending team.

B. Personal Foul.

A Player Shall Not—

SEC. 11. Hold, block, trip, charge or push an opponent.

SEC. 12. Use unnecessary roughness.

List of
Personal
Fouls.

PENALTY— (SECTIONS 11, 12.)
Free trial for goal. The offender shall be charged also with a personal foul. The Referee may disqualify for a single violation of Sec. 11 or 12.

SEC. 13. ˊ Push or hold an opponent who is in the act of throwing for the basket.

PENALTY— (SECTION 13.)
Two free trials. The offender shall be charged with one personal foul and may be disqualified.

NOTE—If the goal is made it counts and the two free throws are also allowed.

C. Disqualifications.

A player who has committed *five technical fouls,* or *four personal fouls,* or a sum total of *six fouls, either technical or personal,* is automatically disqualified and removed from the game.

New Ruling.

In all cases not covered by the rules, officials are to use their own judgment in accordance with the general spirit of the rules.

Inquiries on interpretations of rules should be addressed to Mr. George T. Hepbron, 45 Rose Street, New York City.

Method of Scoring Basketball

Any coach who is interested in good basketball should keep all scores in a uniform way, and preferably in a score book. Only in this way is it possible to keep track of the playing of your team—their propensity to make fouls, and the fouls they most commonly make. It also shows the good playing of your team members; if a forward makes many baskets and few fouls, she is a good player, and if a guard makes few fouls and she has prevented the opponents from making many baskets, she is a good player. A score book also shows the history of the playing of the team. One can look back months or years, and see whether such playing has improved and how it has improved. Below will be found a sample score blank. It has been filled out in the manner usually employed by scorers of men's games, and, if adopted, will make a uniform system of scoring the game of basketball. Let us take the scoring of the first half of the game on the sample score card. Ada Brown has made a goal from the field, two goals from the foul line and one goal from a two-hand overhead shot. Mary Robinson made a goal from the foul line and missed a goal from the foul line, etc. Susan Smith made two fouls—both technical. Helen Peters made one personal and one technical foul, etc. The score at the end of the first half for 1922 was 6 points. It is also interesting to note how one is able to follow up the fouls of one team by goals or attempts at goals from the foul line.

Class of 1922

Position	Names of Players	First Half	Second Half
Forwards	Ada Brown	X ⊗ ⊗ ⊙	⊗ ⊗
Forwards	Mary Robinson	⊗ ○	X X ○ X
Centers	Susan Smith	T1 T2	T3
Centers	Helen Peters	P1 T1	·
Guards	Fay Calhoun	P1	T1 T2
Guards	Eva Strong	T1	
		6	8

Class of 1923

Position	Names of Players	First Half	Second Half
Forwards	Marion May	X ⊗ ○	⊙ T X
Forwards	Lucy Conolo	⊗ ⊗	X ⊗ ○
Centers	Jane True	T1	
Centers	Lily Bray		
Guards	Bessie Bee		
Guards	Dora Day		T1
		5	7

WHERE PLAYED *Girls' School* DATE *Mar. 15, 1921* REFEREE *Miss Wheeler* UMPIRE *Miss Smith*

TIMEKEEPERS *E. Davis – A. Bruce* SCORERS *A. Coe – B. Lee* LINESMEN *W. Clark – C. Blue* WON BY *Class of 1922* SCORE *14–12*

HOW TO SCORE: To score a field goal, mark an X; for a two-hand overhead shot, a dot in a circle; for a goal from the foul line, an X in a circle; for a missed goal from the foul line, a plain circle. Personal fouls should be marked P1, P2, etc., and technical fouls, T1, T2, etc. For list of fouls and their penalties, see Rule 15.

Index to Rules

* Indicates that the Note which follows the Section is referred to.

Questions and Answers

COMPILED BY G. T. HEPBRON.

Inquiries on interpretations of rules should be addressed to George T. Hepbron, Secretary, 45 Rose Street, New York, N. Y.

Always enclose a self-addressed stamped envelope for reply. Number each paragraph in your letter. Ask only one question in each paragraph stating rule and section involved.

If you desire reply on sheet enclosed, this can be done only if a duplicate accompanies the original.

If your questions are framed and numbered so that "Yes" or "No" will suffice for answer it will facilitate a quick reply.

Question No. 1. Suppose the Timekeeper is not provided with a suitable horn or bell and is therefore unable to make Referee hear her call "time" orally and a goal is made, does it count? *Answer*—Yes; the game is officially in progress until proper signal is sounded either by the Timekeeper or Referee. See Rule 6, Sec. 12.

Question No. 2. Two players are jumping for ball being tossed up by Referee; one player bats ball into opponents' basket; does the goal count and for whom? *Answer*—Goal counts for team into whose basket it was batted. See Rule 7, Sec. 1.

Question No. 3. Ball glances off face of backboard and across boundary line, but before it touches the floor or any obstruction out of bounds, it is caught by a player who has both feet "in bounds." Is the ball in bounds or out of bounds? *Answer*—In bounds. See Rule 7, Sec. 2.

Question No. 4. Would standing still and bouncing the ball on the floor constitute a dribble? *Answer*—Yes. See Rule 7, Sec. 7.

Question No. 5. May a player dribble the ball without it touching the floor? *Answer*—A dribble to be legal must come in contact with the floor. See Rule 7, Sec. 7; Rule 15, Sec. 5.

Question No. 6. Some guards have the habit of putting their hands on body of opponent; is this a violation of the rules? *Answer*—It certainly is; a personal foul should be called for "holding." See Rule 7, Sec. 19c and 20.

Question No. 7. When the ball is tossed up by the Referee in center or elsewhere, are both players obliged to jump and make an effort to tap the ball? *Answer*—Yes. If neither player taps the ball, the Referee shall toss it up again at the same place and order both players to jump and make an honest attempt to tap it. Failure to comply with the Referee's order is a foul on one or both for delaying the game. See Rule 8, Sec. 9, and Rule 7, Sec. 12.

Question No. 8. Must the players face toward their "own" baskets when jumping in center or elsewhere? *Answer*—No particular facing is required, provided each player is in own half of circle. See Rule 8, Sec. 8B and 10.

Question No. 9. When ball is tapped after jumping in center or elsewhere, can either one or both jumpers touch it again before it is touched by a third player? *Answer*—Yes; retapped, but not caught. See Rule 8, Sec. 11.

Question No. 10. Ball is being tossed up by Referee between two players; after it has been tapped and before any other player touches it, it goes to "out of bounds"; Referee is undecided which player touched it last; what is the decision? *Answer*—See Rule 8, Sec. 9; Rule 10, Sec. 2.

Question No. 11. When players are jumping for ball tossed up by Referee elsewhere than in the center, do the same conditions prevail as when jumping in center? *Answer*—Yes. See Rule 8, Sec. 9, 10 and 11.

Question No. 12. May a player dribble the ball while part of her person is touching the floor out of bounds, without violating the rules? *Answer*—No. See Rule 7, Sec. 2; Rule 10, Sec. 1, and Rule 14, Sec. 4 and 5.

Question No. 13. Two players have possession of ball, third player runs in, personal contact results, but third player does not touch ball; what is the decision? *Answer*—Personal foul against third player. See Rule 15, Sec. 11 and 12.

Question No. 14. What is the penalty for holding arm or shoulder of an opponent who is in the act of trying for goal? *Answer*—Two free trials for goal from free throw line. See Rule 15, Sec. 13.

Question No. 15. A player is dribbling and an opponent runs in at right angles to the direction the dribbler is going and bats the ball, and while so doing personal contact results; has a foul been committed, and on which one? *Answer*—A foul for personal contact has been committed; it may have been the fault of either; the official who decides must see the play to make decision; the burden of proof, however, is on the dribbler.

Question No. 16. May the personal foul rules (Rule 15, Sec. 11 to 13) be set aside by mutual agreement? *Answer*—Decidedly not; the personal foul rule is intended to prevent the most flagrant fouls in the game. Strict rulings on these points will do much to keep the game clean. It is the urgent desire of the Committee that all rules be strictly enforced in their entirety, especially those relating to personal fouls.

Question No. 17. When players are jumping for ball being tossed up by the Referee, whether in center or elsewhere, may either one or both players catch the ball after it has been tapped, before it is touched by a third player? *Answer*—Yes, provided it has touched the floor. See Rule 8, Sec. 11.

Question No. 18. May a player step onto the second line when the field lines are double? *Answer*—Yes, provided she does not step *beyond*. See Rule 7, Sec. 22, and Rule 14, Sec. 7.

Question No. 19. A line violation is made, the ball progresses some distance before the whistle is blown; is the ball returned to the spot where its violation was made? *Answer*—No. It is given to the member of the opposing team nearest the spot where the ball was at the time the whistle was blown. If the linesmen keep their whistles constantly between their lips, this will not occur. See Rule 14, Sec. 7A.

Question No. 20. Is it a foul to hug the ball? *Answer*—Hugging the ball is not a foul.

Question No. 21. Suppose one player is forced "out of bounds" by an opponent, what is the decision? *Answer*—Foul on opponent who did the forcing.

Question No. 22. Is it legal to guard a player who is trying for goal from the field as closely as at other times? *Answer*—Yes; personal contact is illegal at all times, whether committed on player trying for goal or otherwise.

Question No. 23. Is it an illegal play to catch the ball against the body? *Answer*—No.

Question No. 24. The Scorers fail to notify the Referee that a player has committed the number of personal or technical fouls which would disqualify her and she continues to play; what should be done? *Answer*—The points made during the period that this player was ineligible shall be counted as well as the time played, but immediate substitution for offending player shall be made as soon as the fact that she has four personal fouls or five technical fouls, or a total of six personal and technical fouls combined, comes to the attention of the official. If Scorers are so inefficient or negligent that they fail to notify the Referee, they should be at once removed from that game and not permitted to serve in any capacity for the remainder of the season. No excuses should be accepted.

Question No. 25. If a court is too small to use outside boundary lines, what ground rules would you suggest? *Answer*—Use whole court as playing space. In this case there can be no "out-of-bounds."

Question No. 26. Suppose a team has no substitutes and a player is disqualified, is the team obliged to play short or is the game awarded to opponents? *Answer*—Play short if no agreement was entered into before game.

The Duties of Basketball Officials

By L. Raymond Burnett, M.D.,
Superintendent City Recreation. Paterson, N. J.

Basketball is the most universal indoor game and has increased in popularity very rapidly since the general adoption of uniform rules. In every locality where women's basketball has been allowed to languish, it will be found that poor officiating has been the underlying cause. Ignorance of the rules or lack of backbone to strictly enforce them has caused much of the unfavorable opinion among those school authorities who do not encourage the game. They have allowed match games without proper management and have not inquired into the reasons for unsportsmanlike contests.

Women should usually manage all games played by girls, and there is no reason why their work should not be as efficient as that of the most experienced men. It is a fact, however, that the game has become popular in many cities without a corresponding growth in the number of competent women officials. Many successful physical directors are not good officials simply because they do not make a thorough study of the rules, while others are satisfied with their work when they merely toss the ball and then remain standing near the center until a goal is made.

The various normal schools for physical education are rapidly developing competent officials by giving careful instruction in the technique; but, even in such schools, a large proportion of the candidates are not physically or mentally equipped to become expert referees.

The referee of a basketball game needs a quicker reaction time and greater physical endurance than in any other contest, unless it be in cross ball, which is an outdoor game played with two basketballs. She must follow the ball closely and recognize fouls instantly, having played the game herself often enough to analyze the players' thoughts.

COSTUME.

No one should attempt to referee while dressed in the ordinary street costume. as skirts and leather-soled shoes prevent following the ball about the court. A referee in high-heeled shoes and wearing a picture hat has been seen at an important game, and when the ball had to be tossed, she delayed the game while hobbling to position. Regular gymnasium costume, differing in color from that of the players and allowing perfect freedom, is the most practical dress. Rubber-soled shoes are a necessity for a proper covering of the court, since a good official in a fast game must run and walk constantly for thirty minutes. An official wearing a pedometer during a match game at the Harvard Summer School traveled two and three-quarter miles.

PHYSICAL CONDITION.

Such officiating requires a physical condition equal to that of the players, and there is no better way to attain this training than to play often in the practice games of some team. Referee other practice games, keeping always near the ball, as this keeps the game fast and clean while the players go at top speed. When the players and onlookers realize that you intend to be near every play from the early minutes of the game, you will have gained their confidence and co-operation. Your quick, impartial decisions. made almost before they have formulated their own opinions of plays, will soon establish your reputation.

KNOWLEDGE OF THE RULES.

For many years, since the invention of the game in 1892, we have had several sets of rules for basketball; and at one time it was necessary to study seven printed guides, with variations, in order to instruct coaches in a summer school, who needed to know the local differences.

This Guide contains the revised official rules published with the authority of the American Physical Education Association, so it is now only necessary to know how the men's game differs from these rules. Such radical differences are present that different names for the games would cause less confusion. One should never take it for granted that a good knowledge of the men's rules will assure success with the women's rules after five minutes' study.

Commit these rules to memory so that the exact wording will be "at your tongue's end" when a point for decision arises. Such a knowledge will give you prestige as one who knows her business. Always have the rules available to verify statements, and know how to use the index so that little delay will occur. Try to attend all meetings of coaches in your vicinity where rule interpretations are discussed. Organize coaches in associations if you live where none exist. All doubtful points may be cleared up by sending a self-addressed envelope enclosed with the question to the Rules Committee.

PRELIMINARIES.

Since the referee in match games is usually secured by the manager, you may not see the players until a few minutes before play commences. Get acquainted with the captains and call both teams into a corner or a small room for a short talk; tell them in a quiet way that you expect to strictly enforce the rules without regard to sides. Explain any changes in ground rules and ask for questions regarding interpretation of the guarding fouls, or have all of the pictures taken from the Guide and mounted upon a card so that they may be readily shown and discussed. Tell them that your whistle stops the game and that whoever has the ball should pass it to you at once when in doubt, so that you may announce the decision without loss of playing time. This five-minute talk will start you as a friend of the individual players on both teams.

The scorers and timekeepers are your assistants and should be seated near the middle of the side lines, not at one end or separate. You often wish to speak to them while passing down the court during play. In answer to their questions regarding the player who fouled and the score. Explain to the scorers that you will raise an arm above your head and indicate the score by extended fingers while announcing the score distinctly to the spectators. You will also look toward them and indicate a personal foul by fully extending an arm upward.

Allow only one score book to be used during the game, so that both scorers may watch one set of figures. A duplicate copy can be easily made for the visiting team or reporters after the game. Much confusion occurs when the scorers attempt to keep separate records and do not know the individual players.

TIMEKEEPERS' DUTIES.

See that the timers know how to stop and start the stopwatch and that they have a separate watch for keeping the "time out" taken for delays. When, as often happens, a stopwatch is not available, the timers' duties become very difficult; in fact, absolute accuracy, to the second, is impossible. With an ordinary watch, each delay makes two problems in arithmetic, which should be done on paper by the assistant timer. This is best done by noting the minute and second when the game would stop if there were no delays, and then adding to this the seconds and minutes taken out for each delay. A well equipped court should have a six-inch wall-gong within reach of the timer.

LINESMEN.

Then make the acquaintance of the linesmen and see that they have suitable positions at the ends of the division lines and are equipped with whistles. They should know that a player can step upon or in the twelve-inch neutral space, but cannot touch the ground beyond; and that when two narrow lines are used, they are supposed to measure twelve inches over all. Suggest that the space between be temporarily marked with wet chalk. A player has not technically committed a line violation if she leaps across the corner of the adjacent division to out of bounds, in order to prevent falling over the division line.

It is often necessary to make a statement to the spectators crowded under a goal or seated in a gallery near the backboards, since they must keep three feet or more away from the goals.

When the spectators are standing or seated near the boundaries, the referee should ask that the ball be not caught or batted by them.

If there are any special ground rules necessary because of projecting obstructions, or a shortened time because the game started late, these should be announced to players and spectators before the game, to prevent disagreements later.

In your talk with the captains, make sure that they understand that substitutes must report to you, so that you may announce the substitution with name, position and team. The captains are the only ones who should converse with any official during the playing time.

DIFFICULT DECISIONS.

The most frequent foul in women's rules is that of overguarding an opponent who has the ball. Then come running with the ball, delaying the game, and rough play. You must have a clear mental picture of legal guarding with the arms in vertical plane, and be ready to illustrate if your strictness or judgment is questioned. A player cannot reach forward or place an arm around an opponent's body while guarding from behind, and this relative position occurs constantly because a good player with the ball turns her back upon the nearest opponent.

Making progress with the ball is clearly defined in these rules. Many nervous players make short sideward steps unconsciously while holding the ball and are surprised when the foul is called.

Delay of the game may be due to holding the ball too long either in the court or out of bounds, in taking more than ten seconds to attempt a free throw, in failing to get upon the feet quickly while holding the ball, and in failure to get into position quickly when the ball is to be tossed.

The players and spectators size up your ability in the first few minutes of play, and if you have called the first fouls strictly they know that you are not to be trifled with, and the game becomes fast and clean.

You should announce a double foul by indicating the offenders and calling "time out" to the timers. As there is no advantage in the first free throw, you should get the ball and place it upon the nearest free throw line without delay; then stand near the goal to secure it after the throw and carry it to the other free throw line.

When the ball goes out of bounds, you should instantly blow the whistle and indicate the player entitled to it by calling "Red out," or the team name, since each player must know in order to develop team play.

COUNTING FOR HELD BALL.

Begin counting aloud the five seconds limit as soon as the player has the ball and is standing at right angles to where the ball went over the line, remembering that she need not come up close to the line to be in position. A person ordinarily counts ten in five seconds, so you must practice counting five seconds while observing the second hand on a watch. This is important, because you must frequently count three seconds accurately while the player has the ball in bounds. Making a practice of counting aloud will speed up the game when you discover that certain players are inclined to delay passing, and for the last count substitute the whistle blast calling the foul. Note that a wise player may really hold the ball almost six seconds by putting in the one juggle or bounce, and these plays need counting.

THE WHISTLE.

The best make of whistle for women's use is the deep two-toned whistle with short chain for attachment to the clothing. The shrill-toned whistle with cork ball is not so distinctly heard when a feminine group is cheering a fast game, but this sort of whistle may be used by the umpire and lines-

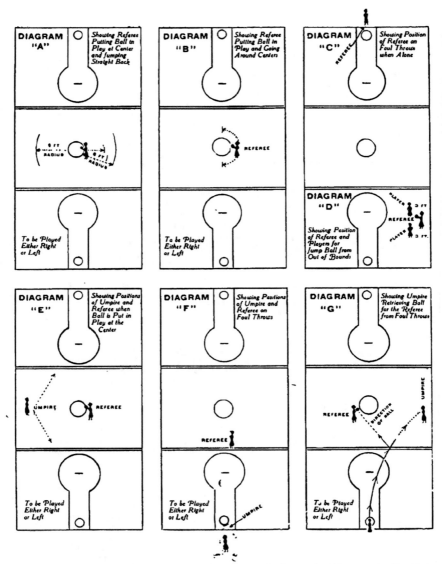

Diagram "A" shows the limit of distance the Referee should move in the first few seconds after tossing ball. Diagram "B" represents a Referee who dodges the player by stepping behind the weaker of two jumpers. Diagram "C" shows Referee out of bounds. Diagram "D" emphasizes that Referee should be nearer the wall than are the jumpers. Diagram "E" shows Umpire covering opposite side from Referee. Diagram "F." Here the Umpire assists the Referee by standing out of bounds. Diagram "G." This carry of the ball by the Umpire results when a foul goal is thrown.

men. The timer should be furnished with a horn or gong. The whistle should be carried between the lips for instant use, except when counting, and especially when tossing the ball between two players, both hands being needed to make an accurate vertical toss.

When two players hold a ball or you do not know who touched it last before it went out of bounds, blow the whistle and call "Tie ball" or "Jump."

PUTTING THE BALL IN PLAY.

Make a practice of tossing the ball always the same height. Do not follow the ball up with your eyes, but watch the jumpers and whistle when you know the ball is beyond their reach.

a. AT THE CENTER. The referee when tossing the ball at center, should stand in a triangle with the players and hold the ball between them, thus preventing too close playing. Note that five feet are in the ring, counting one of yours, and that each of the centers has a hand in contact with her back. When the ball leaves your hands, take one quick step backward, then another slow one, thus avoiding the center play, without getting in the way of circling side-centers. Running off the court will surely cause interference. Your judgment should tell you where to step after the ball is in play. This position is shown in "A" of the diagrams, which are modeled after those in the invaluable article by Homer S. Curtis in Spalding's Official 1917 Basketball Guide for Men.

Diagram "B" shows another position at center which the referee can occasionally take after the toss. You have discovered that one center always taps the ball forward and runs sideward and that the side-center will not be interfered with if you step around behind this center. Such a move gives you an opportunity to enforce the rule of "Hand behind the back" on both centers.

b. FROM OUT OF BOUNDS. Diagram "D" represents the relative position of the jumping players and referee when the ball is brought in from out of bounds or has been held in tie within bounds. You should secure the ball and stand with back to the nearest side line, making the players come to the spot which you indicate. Toss the ball with both hands and step instantly out of the zone of play, which means out of bounds when possible.

REFEREE'S POSITION DURING FOUL THROWS.

Diagram "C" shows where the referee should stand when you are the only official and there is space for you to stand out of bounds. The rules require the referee to secure the ball and immediately place it upon the foul line of the offended side or hand it to the thrower if she is already standing upon this line. This is a good rule to speed up the game and a point where it previously has been full of delays, and you should begin counting the ten seconds aloud, only continuing silently when the thrower begins her aim or throwing motion. This ruling has been in force in men's rules for some time, but many officials do not begin counting at the instant when the ball is placed upon the line, as the rules require, but wait until the thrower has come to the line. Such delay is really the fault of the official, and captains must be instructed to have their free thrower selected before the penalty is awarded, since if more than ten seconds are taken to decide, there will be no throw to try.

The ball is in play after a missed free throw, so your position under the goal will allow you to watch the scrimmage and you can readily tell when the ball or player goes out of bounds. Your position here, facing the players, will tend to make them observe the free throw lane and prevent crowding. If the goal is made and no line violations have occurred, you should catch the ball as it drops from the basket and hasten to the center for the next toss, passing close by the scorer and announcing the score to the spectators. At the end of the half it is often wise to hold a short conference with the captains, asking their criticism and offering to explain any interpretation which may have been made. Do not get chummy with any players at this time, as the other team might think of favoritism.

Finally, the referee should not consider herself a policeman, a coach, nor a spectator. The referee's sole duties are to interpret the rules and carry on the game without delay.

DUTIES OF THE UMPIRE.

The common practice of alternating the duties of the referee and umpire, at the end of the first half in women's basketball, has no place in the rules of the game, but is done as a matter of courtesy. This has given rise to the impression in the minds of many good players that the umpire is a supernumerary official who merely acts as a check for poor refereeing. Really, the two officials are necessary, and their duties are distinct. They should work together to make a fast, clean game, enjoyable to players and spectators. The umpire can call all fouls, but should especially watch the players away from the ball, since the referee has particular charge of the action about the ball. You cannot consider yourself a competent umpire if you stand or sit on one side and occasionally call a double foul when the referee has designated but one offender. You should assist the referee on out of bounds decisions, not by blowing a whistle and announcing the side, but by quietly indicating to the referee the player who is entitled to the ball when the referee would otherwise toss it up. Your whistle should be held between the lips and you should take a position facing the referee at the start of the game, as in Diagram "E." When the referee starts toward one end following the ball, you should travel the other way and at all times command a view of the court remote from the referee. At each toss you again assume a position on the opposite side from the referee. Although you will not cover so much ground as the referee, by constant shifting you will enable the referee to follow the ball more closely.

Diagram "F" shows the best positions for referee and umpire during free throws. The umpire will be located under the goal, as the referee was when officiating alone. The referee should stand upon the neutral line behind the thrower and observe the throw. When the goal is made, the umpire secures the ball and, as illustrated in Diagram "G," runs with it toward the center and makes a short pass to the referee, who is already in position for another toss. When this team work is promptly done, the officials are invariably ready and waiting for the players, instead of waiting for some spectator to throw the ball to center.

The umpire can often retrieve balls from out of bounds quicker than the player who is entitled to it, and this always should be done to speed up the game. There is little danger of over-speeding the game, now that four quarters with three regular rest periods are used.

When both officials call fouls upon one player, the penalty for the graver offense should be the one enforced. A "line violation" could never take precedence over "delay of the game," but a "personal contact" foul always would be more important than one for "making progress with the ball."

Every coach should try to select two or more persons who are interested in the game, although not regular players, for training as officials. The best officials are not always star players. A coach should rarely, if ever, referee a match game of her own team. The suspicion of partiality cannot be eliminated, although the coach may be competent in knowledge of rules, physically fit, prompt in making accurate decisions at the cost of popularity, and possesses the ideals of a perfect sportsman. It is a worthy work to teach a team to "win if they can fairly, but lose gracefully if they must."

The development of a good official needs the experience of several seasons, and the average official may not fully meet the ideals set forth in this article; but every point understood will improve the conduct of our national indoor game.

How to Coach Beginners

BY MISS ELIZABETH RICHARDS, SMITH COLLEGE, NORTHAMPTON, MASS.

Basketball, properly played, requires mental alertness and physical skill. It requires the mental ability to see the most effective way of meeting a situation, and the physical ability to carry out the idea, once grasped. The basketball coach should, therefore, from the very beginning, aim. to train the players along these very lines of mental alertness and physical ability. Such training can be most effectively gained by combining preliminary practice in throwing, catching, dodging and the like, with the regular playing.

The first requirement is, of course, a swift ball, properly thrown and accurately aimed. This means, especially for girls and women, much coaching and tireless practicing. At the beginning, at least one-quarter of the period should be given over to plain "ball throwing." This may be done in several ways, such as:

1—Standing in a circle, with the coach in the center. The coach can then throw different types of balls, overhand, underhand, side, high, etc., and ask that the ball be returned in the same manner as thrown. This gives the players practice in both catching and throwing. The circle may be made larger or smaller, as desired, to gain different throwing distances.

2—Still in the circle formation, with coach in center, the players advance, running around the circle. This gives the players practice in catching the ball while running. The players should be taught to always jump to reach the ball and to land firmly on two feet—remaining there for a second while throwing the ball. Much "running with the ball" will be prevented if players can once gain this habit of jumping and landing on both feet.

3—Passing the ball in games arranged in line formation—teacher ball, line relay, etc.

The point next taken up should be the passing of the ball between players, with some opposition. This is gained most effectively in some institutions by what is termed "end practice," and is given as follows:

The teams are lined up against each other, and a coach is appointed for each of the three field sections. These coaches need not all be professional coaches. Upper class students, captains, etc., may be very helpful. The coach stands on the field line facing her section, ball in hand, and calls for a certain player to receive the ball. This player must then by quick dodging get in front of the opponent and catch the ball from the coach. Dropping back is a poor play and should be discouraged. Getting in front of one's opponent means quicker passes and cleaner playing.

At first in end practice the player should pass the ball directly back to the coach. Later the player should receive the ball from the coach and pass it on to another player, thus working it to the goal or field line. As soon as a team is ready for definite passes, they should be practiced in the time given to end practice. This end practice cannot be overestimated. It teaches quickness of response, catching, throwing. dodging and team play. It enables the coach to work with only a few players and hence allows almost individual instruction. It will teach the players the value of working together, staying in their respective positions, and not massing in a helter-skelter mob over the ball.

Another excellent way of obtaining team play is by what is known as "skeleton practice." This is done by having one team up at a time. and, by a series of passes, working the ball down the field. If the games are to be interclass, each class should have two or three passes, unknown to the other classes; if interschool, each school may work up its own passes.

In this skeleton practice the team is lined up, without opposition, and the ball is started at different points, the whole team acting to work it through. The following pass may serve as an example: The ball is started

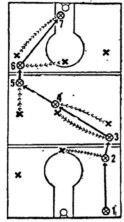

at the back line by the guard (No. 1); it is passed to the center guard, who runs over to the corner near the field line to receive it (No. 2); at the same time the center center has run over to the right and up to the field line, and there, as No. 3 receives the ball from No. 2, the right side center drops into the center (No. 4), receives the ball and passes it to the left side center (No. 5), who has run ahead to the next field line, thus giving a straight diagonal pass across center. The center forward runs up to the line to receive the ball (No. 6), and the left forward drops back near the basket (No. 7) and there receives the ball and tries for goal. This is, therefore, a definite team play, a series of passes, worked out ahead of time, and planned to enable a team to outwit its opposition by playing in an unexpected way, instead of the usual obvious manner.

Any number of these passes might be worked out, and a team which knows a few good passes and can apply them will be very apt to get ahead of the opposing team. For the skeleton practice, the team should be lined up, first without opposition, and the ball should be quickly passed down the field in the manner desired until each player knows the pass and can use it intelligently. Then it should be tried out with opposition, simply working out the pass from guard to forward, so that it may later be successfully used in the game.

The forwards should be taught that much depends upon them. A goal made always inspires a team to better playing. The forwards should have certain signals and passes well worked out and known to all three. No one should try for the position of forward who is unwilling to spend many hours alone in the field, simply trying for the basket—cultivating aim, accuracy and precision. This can be gained only by constant practice and cannot be overemphasized.

The foregoing does not, of course, begin to cover all of the details which the coach must remember in coaching beginners. They are merely *aids* in *methods* of coaching. Slowness, rough play, overguarding, etc., must be constantly spoken of, and individual quickness and cleanness of playing constantly encouraged.

Also, the coach must remember that a liking for the game is the first essential. Do not overload a beginner with too many technicalities. Get some fun and speed into the game, and then slow it down later on. Different players demand different treatment. Older players will be more keen for the scientific game at an early stage. With any set of people it is wise to always finish the practice with a "real" game. Use the ball throwing, skeleton practice and end practice as much as possible to train accurate and skillful playing, and then keep the enthusiasm and interest of the players by a few moments of "real" play, even though it may at first seem rough and confused. As soon as players have advanced a bit, the throwing practice may be eliminated. End practice is useful for a much longer time, and skeleton practice or the working out of well planned passes will always benefit a team.

Make for good spirit and good clean playing from the very beginning, and the foundation is laid for good sportsmanship and high standards for all time.

The Beneficial Results and the Dangers of Basketball

BY DR. J. ANNA NORRIS.

The most popular indoor game in a girls' gymnasium is basketball. Its vigorous competitive spirit, its opportunities for individual brilliant play coupled with its necessity for controlled team work, its rapidity, its joyousness and its resultant feeling of well-being, all contribute to this situation.

Physiologically it has the advantage of securing widespread hygienic results without a disproportionate demand on the heart. This is accomplished because it requires the activity of large groups of muscles for a moderate length of time without requiring maximum effort of any one of them.

Its first noticeable physiological result is the quickening and intensifying of the heart action and of the breathing. This indicates that the heart and lungs are being called on to hasten the withdrawal from the blood of the large amount of carbon dioxide which is being thrown into it by work of the muscles. A condition of breathlessness after exercise shows that the heart is having difficulty in keeping up its end of the work, and if not relieved by respite it may prove unequal to the task. In this case a condition of "strain" may ensue. In the untrained person this sign of heart embarrassment may occur very promptly during strenuous exercise.

It should go without saying that a medical examination should be a prerequisite for anyone who wishes to enter a basketball class or squad, in order to make sure that no organic weakness exists which would be aggravated by such vigorous exertion. But in addition to this, if the girl is untrained physically, the instructor should be keen to observe conditions of breathlessness as stated above, because of its being an indication of heart embarrassment. Without doubt, untrained hearts which are sound will increase in strength and in quickness of reaction ·to exercise, if only they may be allowed time for growing stronger. This may be accomplished in basketball by playing for very short periods of time: e. g., by playing quarters instead of halves, or by sending the breathless ones out to rest for a few minutes, and by keeping the total time of practice strictly within hygienic limits.

The observation for this latter purpose should not be confined to the gymnasium floor, but should include a report as to whether the girl is more tired later in the day, or too tired to study in the evening, when she should be better fitted for clear thought as a result of her vigorous exercise. It is not enough to secure a statement as to whether she feels tired at the end of the practice, for her exhilaration of feeling may blind her to fatigue. Report from her home that she is over-tired on the evenings after she has played basketball should result in shortening her periods of playing, and may occasionally make it necessary for her to give it up and substitute some milder form of exercise.

The restrictions imposed by the official rule which divides the field into three courts has done so much to eliminate heart strain, that many a girl can play the game safely now and will grow stronger by it, who, under the old rules, would not have been permitted to play at all.

Another important hygienic result of basketball comes from the use of the big muscles of the trunk in bending and twisting and the upward movement of the arms in throwing the ball. The permanent uplift of the ribs and the broadening of the subcostal angle afford added room for the vital organs, while the strengthening of muscles of abdomen and loins gives support to the organs. The strengthening of the back muscles goes far toward banishing backache and tired feelings.

All the good results of stimulating the lymph flow, which come from deep breathing and muscular contraction and joint action, are gained par excellence through basketball. Irritations, nervousness, tenseness, headaches, tired feelings and other results of indoor lives accompanied by mental and emotional stress, may be sent a-glimmering by a properly conducted game if the individual has the organic strength for it.

It always must be remembered that the fascination of the game is so great, and the sense of responsibility to the team in a match game is so strong, that there is temptation to play at the time of menstruation.* Strict rules should be made, and if possible the public sentiment of the school should be so strongly developed in favor of living by them that the captains of the teams may be entrusted with enforcing them. One of the good reasons for employing women to teach basketball is that they can talk with the players regarding this matter with entire frankness.

The nervous strength of a girl should be considered with great care when choosing players for a class team. The strain of a championship interclass game is so much greater than that of ordinary playing, that a girl who is lacking in nervous poise may go to pieces under it. The loss of confidence following such a breakdown of morale is a real detriment to any girl and she should not be subjected to it. On the other hand, if she realizes that calm mental poise is going to count heavily in her chances for making a team, she may put herself under a stricter discipline than if no prize were in view, and the educational effect will be most helpful.

When one comes to speaking more in detail of the educational results of basketball, there are many benefits to be found accruing from it; in fact, it is educationally one of the most important games that exist for adolescent girls. It makes a call that is as insistent as in any of the less highly organized games, for alertness, accuracy, observation of rules, training of the eye and of general co-ordination, and in addition it can teach invaluable lessons in the socially important virtues of good sportsmanship, loyalty and team play. That it does not always do so is a reflection on the spirit of the instructor, not on the game.

It is quite possible for it to foster a spirit of boisterousness and mannishness, and this is especially likely to crop out if match games with other institutions are played, or if newspapers over-emphasize the event, or if games are played before audiences that treat them as spectacles. In such cases, not only is self-display likely to creep in, but the rivalry may become a bitter antagonism, so that good comradeship between opposing teams may be absent, and the lessons are lost that might have been learned by accepting either victory or defeat with dignity. The danger of the development of the wrong attitude is one of the strong reasons brought forward against permitting interscholastic games.

But if the game is strictly and amiably and helpfully refereed, and if it has been taught in the spirit of good sportsmanship, it has splendid lessons to enforce. The quick action in emergency, the cool thought in trying circumstances, the keeping of temper when losing or when accidentally jostled, the perseverance when the odds are against one, the forgetfulness of self in the attempt to perfect team play—all these educational experiences must tend in the direction of improving the girl's attitude toward her fellow workers in later life and toward making her a better co-operating member of society. Much as we esteem the game for its value in helping to build up vigor and endurance, we consider that its function in disciplining the vigorous young people who can play it gives it a prime claim to the popularity in which it is held by the teachers as well as by the taught.

*It is accepted by most authorities that there should be no basketball during at least three days at this time.

Women's versus Men's Basketball Rules

BY HAZEL H. PRATT,

Director of Athletics for Women, University of Kansas.

At the present time the value of athletics for women as a means of health, recreation and education is gradually being recognized by educators and is being given a place in our school curriculum. One big factor in the retardation of the development of athletics has been the lack of a standard. Whenever women have taken part in the same athletic games as men they have been compared with them; and as they are not world record-breakers, they suffer by comparison.

Basketball is the most popular athletic game for women, yet she cannot play according to the men's interpretation of the game and receive the most benefit. There are certain fundamental sex differences which cannot be disregarded.

First, there is a distinct anatomical difference. The women's figure is less mechanically adapted to sports than men. They have a relatively longer trunk, shorter legs, heavier thighs, broader and deeper hips, and the center of gravity lower in the body. They are not built for Marathon runners nor record-breaker high jumpers. Their shoulders are narrower, more sloping, the bones lighter and the lung capacity smaller. They have more adipose tissue and are more liable to serious bruises. They are less muscular, so must resort to skill rather than to brute strength. However, during the past forty years, increased exercise and outdoor life to which women have been admitted have added to their weight, height, lung capacity and physical vigor. Nevertheless, making allowance for their lack of practice and play traditions, they cannot compete in athletic games with men.

Second, a physiological difference. There are rhythmic periods of physical disability when women should have little or no part in athletics. This has a tendency to eliminate highly specialized players as we find them in men's teams. If athletic games have a health value, then we must not have over-development nor over-strain. Physicians claim that basketball has more direct effect upon the development of the heart than any other athletic contest, with the exception of distance running. In preparing to meet the exigencies of life it is normal development that is to be striven for.

Third, a psychological difference. This difference seems to be largely due to the differences in the training of the sexes from infancy to adult years. Through custom, prejudice and tradition the combative instinct in women has not been developed as in men. They are not given the same toys as boys, which have their psychological influence on their mental activity. However, social and industrial systems are demanding that the sterner virtues in women be developed as well as in the men.

Athletic games will increase social and industrial efficiency when adjusted to the fundamental sex differences, yet this adjustment will not detract from the health, recreational and educational values. Unquestionably the essential difference between the men's and women's game of basketball is that the women's game is a non-interference one; that is. two hands being necessary to secure the ball, which prevents snatching and batting it from the hands of another player, and close guarding, which helps to eliminate roughness, falling down and close personal contact. Owing to the fact that their muscles are longer and less hard, without great danger of injury, they cannot stand the strain of an interference game in which physical strength is of as much value as skill.

To illustrate the difference in ruling in the two types of games: In the non-interference game the guarding may be done only with the arms in the vertical position. Furthermore, a "held" or "tie" ball is declared when two opposing players of opposing teams catch the ball with both hands on the ball. In the interference game a "held" ball is declared when two opposing players of opposing sides have one or both hands on the ball, or when one closely guarded player is unable to throw it. Other important differences iu regulations are :

1. Number of players. A team may consist of from five to nine players. Six is the usual number. Less strain on the center if there is a second center.

2. Playing time lessened. Fifteen-minute halves instead of twenty.

3. The division of the field into three or two parts. The introduction of lines lessens the danger of injury due to physical exhaustion and over-strain. Since women have not had a history of athletic training, it is necessary to minimize the amount of running. The two lines have been introduced at a great educational cost, yet without doubt it is better to sacrifice that phase, if necessary, than health. With adequate training and supervision. the one line game can be developed better to meet the educational, and will meet the health needs of more mature women.

These are the chief differences between the men's and the women's basketball rules. When athletic games are taught and played with equal emphasis placed on their health. recreational and educational values, then, and then only, are we making progress.

The Teaching of Basketball

By Harry Eaton Stewart, M.D.,
New Haven Normal School of Gymnastics.

Basketball is the most highly organized and widely played game that the women and girls in this country enjoy. The scarcity of other good team games enhances its importance in their play life as compared with the athletic life of men and boys. It is then worthy of most careful study and attention that every good feature in it may be so developed as to contribute its utmost to the upbuilding of mental and physical power.

I have purposely used the word "teaching" because it seems more comprehensive from a Normal School standpoint. On no group is the responsibility for carrying on the development of both the spirit and the letter of the game greater than on those who are teaching classes of Normal School students, who in turn become team coaches in such large numbers.

In such teaching three essential points must be borne in mind:

1. The use of the game to teach character building and mental alertness.

2. The acquisition of exact knowledge of the rules and technique of coaching and officiating on the part of the pupil.

3. The further development of the game by a thorough trial of new rules and experimentation with new features to be presented to the committee as changes in the Rules.

Regarding the possibilities of character formation, there is much to be said. I have at every opportunity emphasized this point. Sportsmanship is developed almost entirely by team games. It is an attitude of mind necessary for the well-rounded character of every human being. Women have had until recent years little or no opportunity for acquiring it.

Many opportunities to teach self-control, generosity and self-sacrifice arise in every closely contested game. A good example of such an opportunity for teaching a valuable lesson arose on the occasion of the resumption of games between two schools where friendly competition extended to another sport. The home team was one point ahead in the last minute of play when "time out" was called. The coach of that team took her team from the floor and at the same time gave them instruction, making a total of six technical fouls (this was a five-player team), and thereby made a victory for the visitors certain. Neither coach, principals nor spectators realized that the rules had been infringed. The home team coach was referee, and the visiting coach was umpire of the game—a situation to be avoided whenever possible. The matter was brought to the attention of the referee but not enforced, as it was decided that it was better to lose the game than to take it by a technicality from the team that had played the better game.

Some may not agree with the choice made, but in this case good relations between the schools and the position of the coach may have hung in the balance, and the decision has not been regretted.

The teaching of the technique of the game is most interesting. Careful analysis should be made of the elements that go to make up the different shots, passes and so forth, in order to train the pupils to correct small defects.

More effort should be placed on the training of officials. They are harder to find than players or coaches. The pupils will also learn much in officiating that will help both their playing and coaching.

The Normal Schools are properly the laboratories of the game. It is necessary to teach both the men's rules and the women's rules. The opportunity presented to try out new rules should not be neglected. Let us remain open-minded and ready to try out new methods so that the game may progress in the future as it has in the past, and further increase its great usefulness.

Suggested Rule Changes for 1922-23

By L. Raymond Burnett, M.D.,

Superintendent City Recreation, Paterson, N. J.

The Editorial Committee is open to conviction regarding the ultimate means for perfecting an equalized attack and defense.

The advantage given a forward by the restriction of guarding only in the vertical plane has been a fault of the game for years.

The present rule, which allows only a one-point score for an overhead two-hand throw, is an attempt to create a better balance between defensive and offensive play.

Coaches and teams are urged to try out the following suggestions in prac-tise or interclass games this season:

Draw foul lines; twelve-foot semi-circles about each basket.

Draw one twelve-inch division line on field of any size. This diminishes floor markings from 310 lineal feet to 150 feet, approximately.

Allow forwards to throw the ball in any manner, but score only one point if thrower touches within semi-circle while scoring or in recovering balance after a throw which results in a goal.

After a foul, allow a free throw from any point at least twelve feet from basket, and players of both sides must stay outside of semi-circle until throw is made.

Use a team of six players with three forwards and three guards, allowing a guard to act as jumping center without crossing the division line. This formation allows three forwards to execute any triangle play possible in men's rules and eliminates the necessity for distinctive colors on roving centers.

Among the advantages claimed are:

1. The ease with which temporary floor markings can be accurately placed.

2. The premium placed upon scoring from a distance of twelve feet, thus reducing the congestion of players under the basket. With the present rules, the players often bunch under the goal because the majority of scoring throws are made from the easiest throwing areas, which are four feet to the right and left of the basket.

3. The added incentive to dribble away from the goal when in the one-point area in order to score from twelve feet or more.

4. The desire to score from an overhand throw is diminished because this style is only effective within the semi-circle distance from goal.

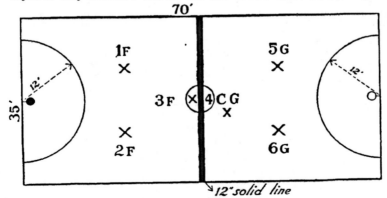

Diagram of field showing one division line with semi-circle used as foul line and to mark area inside of which only one point can be scored. Players are numbered, showing No. 4 as center and guard, thus allowing three forwards. Opponents shown by X.

Basketball in the University and College

BY MISS HELEN FROST, TEACHERS' COLLEGE, COLUMBIA UNIVERSITY.

The phrase "basketball in the college" brings to mind the setting of the game and the related problems of administration, applied hygiene, recreation for large groups, student organization and coaching, competitive games, *et cetera*. In considering the game itself, one turns naturally to those points which may differentiate college basketball from the game as played by younger girls.

The rules of basketball are the same for high school and college and there should be no difference in their interpretation and spirit, but the individual and team play of the college group may be developed to such an extent that basketball as played by them deserves to be called a senior game. The high school team can play excellent basketball and often outplays the college team because the younger girls are quicker, more agile than their older sisters. The younger girl, however, is apt to play impulsively, to take chances and to rely upon her speed and agility for success in a *limited* style of play. Granting that the college game is often somewhat slower than that played by girls of high school age, it must be more accurate and contain well thought out plays to win for itself a higher place and be considered an advanced type of game.

The college girl should endeavor to perfect a number of passes and shots; she should not attempt many new movements at one time, but gradually extend her play that it may be adequate to the changing situations of the game. The instructor or coach can help the player to a better understanding of how to handle herself and the ball through a study of the mechanics of play; *i. e.*, those principles and movements underlying advantageous throwing, catching, guarding, dodging, pivoting, dribbling, juggling and shooting. Variety of play enables a girl to outwit an opponent who is quicker of movement.

One hears so much about the "natural basketball player." She is usually a girl who has played a long time or one who handles herself easily and without waste motion. Because of her experience in the game or her ease and grace of movement, she is confident in herself and does not restrict her play; she works out her pivot, dodge, dribble and juggle until she can use them with safety. She is able to choose the best pass for a definite situation, and because of the variety of her play her opponent finds it difficult to follow or guard her. Feinting, evading a guard successfully, passing cleanly and with purpose, demand rapid thinking and good judgment, qualities which the college girl can give to the game and by which her individual play may be strengthened and made effective.

Because of the mental qualities she brings to basketball, a high grade of team play can be developed. She will appreciate studying team work to the extent of mapping out her territory, whether it be center, forward or guard, and knowing for each situation in the game her logical position in support of her team mates and in relation to her opponents. The players should study offensive team play; *i.e.*, definite combinations of positions to be played and passes to be made by which the ball progresses toward the goal. It is not enough for the team in possession of the ball to "get free"; each member of the team must anticipate the need for her and be in an advantageous position to further the progress of the ball. Such combinations need not be complicated and they will be limited in number and difficulty by the ability of the individuals making up the team. Signals may be used, but their practice should be encouraged only so far as they improve the quality of the game and do not tend to make it static. The college group is interested in working out its own plays; the mental side of the game has its appeal.

Character Values in Group Games

By MISS MAY S. KISSOCK,

University of Minnesota, Minneapolis.

It has been said that all educators are agreed that the chief purpose of education is the acquiring of an alertness of mind and right mental habits. Let us broaden this statement by adding to right mental habits, right character and social habits. The two are closely allied, for we know from experience that the attitude of mind which is found in play is the attitude which is essential in educating the child or youth, in developing the intellect, the emotions and the will, molding them into the individuals they will eventually become at maturity.

In this article we are concerned chiefly with the play of youth. This is the period when the interest is directed towards games of a more highly organized character than in childhood, where concerted action, co-operation and team play are the chief demands, the period which is the "laboratory of opportunity" for the right formation of character and social traits. In the participation in the group games of this period, we find that the youth is really only sharing in forms of social conduct where there are unlimited opportunities for practice in the same vices and virtues that we find in life.

To be more definite, let us enumerate those right character and social habits which we may reasonably expect to be acquired by this means. If the group games of this period are understandingly and sympathetically led and directed, we ought to find a development in :

1. A sense of justice, honesty and good sportsmanship. This is acquired in two ways—in a tangible fashion, through the strict observance of the rules and regulations of the game and through vigorous punishment of all violations of the rules of the game, whether of the spirit or the letter, and in a more intangible but equally important way, through a continual and constant upholding of the highest ideals in the playing of the game.

2. Determination, where the will to succeed against all obstacles is manifest if properly stimulated and encouraged.

3. Self-control, especially where the games involve personal contact.

4. Loyalty, which is one of the first steps in unselfishness.

5. Fair-mindedness, a respect for the rights and opinions of others.

6. Co-operation and teamwork. Group games necessitate a working together harmoniously of a group of individuals who wish to accomplish a certain thing. This trait is of civic value as well, and is the foundation of democracy.

7. Cheerfulness and modesty, the ability to be a good loser and a magnanimous winner.

Women's basketball played according to women's rules is a splendid illustration of these values which can be obtained in character and social training, provided, as perhaps in no other game, the coach is a leader who does not confine herself merely to directing, but also enters into the spirit of the game with her team ; who not only adheres strictly to the rules, but also interprets them with a sympathetic breadth of vision and an understanding of youth and its needs. Among our young women today no game is played more generally and more enthusiastically than basketball. For this reason we would recommend it as the game best suited to develop in our young women the right character and social habits most essential in education in its broadest sense.

Basketball for Girls and Women

BY MISS ELIZABETH R. STONER.

In time a game proves its value as a sport if it lives to be safe, hygienic, interesting and educational. Basketball for girls and women, after a period of twenty five or thirty years, has undergone many changes. In many cases there was first a feverish stage of playing exactly as men and boys did—five members on a team, no lines of subdivision on the floor, chewing gum "to keep the mouth moist," madly yelling spectators, faking sprains or fainting to secure time to breathe, and other illegal and unsportsmanlike conduct.

Now we have the later development of no basketball tolerated, or nine, seven or six players on a team, students thoroughly examined physically, games perfectly organized and strictly supervised, class or interclass games made up of students who have a passing grade in academic subjects and have passed a posture test.

There is no more interesting game than basketball. It gives a tremendous amount of exercise in a short time; is a test of wits, courage and physique, and develops team-play. It is not so safe a game as volley ball or handball, and unless it is played out-of-doors is not so hygienic as hockey.

The following data received in the spring of 1921 from the high schools and colleges of California, in response to a questionnaire sent to them, answers a number of questions raised about teaching basketball to girls.

The number of high schools reporting was 113.
Colleges reporting, 5.

Spalding rules used in 63 cases.
Spalding women's rules stated, 50.
In 67 cases, physical examinations were required.
In 52 cases, no physical examinations were required.
In 9 high schools the statement was made that the physical instructor supervised.
In 82, there was supervision by a teacher.
In 25, supervision by a coach.
In 3, supervision by a student or a coach.
In 1, supervision by a student.

Length of Practice Time.	No. of Practices per Week.	No. of Players on a Team.
3—15 minutes.	10—1 practice.	8—5 players.
7—20 minutes.	27—4 practices.	87—6 players.
27—30 minutes.	31—2 practices.	3—7 players.
49—45 minutes.	12—5 practices.	15—9 players.
19—60 minutes.	33—3 practices.	1—10 players.
1—1¼ hours.		
4—1½ hours.		

There were different interpretations as to the ruling on lines as follows:

2 stated that they used a two-division court.
18 stated that they used a three-division court.
6, single division lines.
23, double division lines.
3 stated that stepping on the line constituted a foul.
20 gave an unguarded throw for stepping on line.
1 stated that players must be clear across the line before a foul was constituted.
All others referred to the rule book as being the guide.

It is interesting to note that the schools of San Mateo and Santa Clara counties are joined for purposes of sports competition in a Girls' Peninsular Athletic League, in which basketball is the fall feature. Practice games may be played with any schools outside of the two counties. Winners of the League each year are entitled to block letters and the possession of a trophy.

This League recommends to the National Basketball Committee that the rules for each school year should be published by September 1 so that the players do not have to wait until November for the changes. It seems to be the hope of all that physical examination should be required before participation in the game.

Some of the statements which condemned basketball were as follows:

WASCO HIGH SCHOOL—"We consider basketball too trying a game for many high school girls, permit no interschool games, do not encourage the game for girls, and allow only volunteers to play. Physical examinations are not required, but they should be. Practices are 45 minutes, one practice per week, six players on a team."

SANTA BARBARA—"I have absolutely stopped interclass athletics here. Most generally I find the best trained teachers against interscholastic basketball. The more my girls play, the more I am tempted to try it, because it seems a crime that girls cannot be so managed and watched as to do them no harm. Seven players suits us best and we use double lines."

KERN COUNTY UNION HIGH SCHOOL AND JUNIOR COLLEGE, BAKERSFIELD, CAL.—"We consider basketball too strenuous a game to be played by underclassmen (grade schools). Our Junior College and Seniors enjoy the sport now and then. We encourage tennis, hockey and volley ball to take its place."

LINCOLN HIGH SCHOOL, LOS ANGELES—"Since the Los Angeles Board of Education does not permit interscholastic games for girls, we do not play basketball, only as a part of the regular gymnasium period."

COVINA, CAL.—"We are not playing the game this year. Since there are other forms of athletics and gymnastics which are more beneficial and less harmful, we have dispensed with basketball for this year at least."

SAN LUIS OBISPO, CAL.—"We do not play competitive games. Basketball is taught during the regular physical education periods. Great care is used, and girls showing exhaustion are not allowed to continue."

A good point is made by the Polytechnic High School of San Francisco:

"We play with four class teams, each team being allowed to play one game each season with a corresponding team of some other high school. *These games are conducted without spectators*"

I find that the strain comes from the outside and is not the result of the common competition between two teams.

At Reed College, playing basketball was decreased in time to the month of February, one period per week as a sport, but was played in short periods after other activities such as formal gymnastics. At the University of Southern California games are played on a social basis only.

The women of Stanford University, the University of California and Mills College play interclass intercollegiate games when our seasons coincide and permit us to schedule them. The sports included are hockey, handball, rowing, baseball and basketball. This year handball was played by Mills against University of California, hockey against Stanford in the fall, and basketball in March.

The heads of departments of physical education and presidents of the athletic associations of these three colleges have met in the fall of the last two years to arrange schedules, discuss rules, and plan for the year's work in athletics.

Interclass intercollegiate games have proved very interesting, but we find interclass games giving us just as good results—fine enthusiasm for the game and less physical and mental strain afterwards. Not being able to meet the schedule of the challenger, because of local conditions which did not prevail at the time that the year's schedule was made, is liable to cause misunderstandings, and I have seen so many physical training teachers who grew nervous and overcritical during interscholastic games, that I am of the opinion that if we must have interscholastic or intercollegiate games, they should be interclass; but our best, most rational and hygienic plan is to educate our young people to enjoy the games played on a social basis, and thus eliminate all unnecessary physical and mental strain.

West Virginia High School Girls' Basketball Tournament

BY ALBERT C. KELLEY, GRADUATE DIRECTOR.

West Virginia claims the honor of being the first state in the Union to conduct a state high school girls' basketball tournament, and, so far as is known, there is but one other state conducting a girls' tournament at this time—Oklahoma. The West Virginia Tournament originated in 1919 and has been steadily gaining in popularity and numbers since that time. The third annual tournament was held March 10, 11 and 12, 1921, at Spencer, with thirty-three teams, representing as many first-class high schools, in attendance. For three days teams from all sections of the state battled for supremacy, and one by one were eliminated, but only after the most bitter contests. Wheeling High, repeating its 1920 feat, emerged victorious, having defeated Bluefield in the final in a spectacular game. In this connection it might be added that the quintette from the Northern Panhandle combined, in a superb manner, all the qualities that go to make up a first-class team. Their brilliant floor work, uncanny shooting ability and consistent teamwork, spelled defeat for all opponents. Aside from Wheeling there were many other teams of high caliber entered in the 1921 classic, among which may be mentioned Bluefield, Masontown, Sistersville, Warwood, Parkersburg, Huntington, Littleton, Montgomery, Beckley, Follansbee and Triadelphia.

The playing rules of the tournament are Spalding's official rules for women with these changes: Five players only constitute a team; the playing floor is divided into two equal courts by a single line across the center; centers are allowed to play the entire floor and throw for both field and foul goals. The rules as herewith outlined have proved to be ideal for tournament use, as they insure a faster and far more interesting game than would be possible under any other rules, and yet with good officiating the games never become rough. The halves of games throughout the tournament are twelve and a half minutes each, excepting those of finals, whose halves are fifteen minutes. The tournament in West Virginia has marked a new departure in feminine athletics, and its growth from eleven to thirty-three teams in two years is more than proof of its unqualified success.

SPALDING BASKET BALLS

No. **M.** Spalding **Official and Original Basket Ball.** The Spalding No. M was the official ball when the game was originated over twenty-five years ago, and it is to-day the only real official ball because of its quality. The leather in the case—the strongest and most durable possible to produce— is tanned in the Spalding tannery at Leeds, England, and is the same that we also use in our No. J5 official intercollegiate foot ball. Complete with guaranteed rubber bladder, lacing needle and rawhide lace. . . . . Each, **$15.00**

No. M

WE GUARANTEE

every No. M Basket Ball to be perfect in material and workmanship and correct in shape and size when inspected at our factory. If any defect is discovered during the first game in which it is used, or during the first day's practice use, and, if returned at once, we will replace same under this guarantee. We do not guarantee against ordinary wear nor against defect in shape or size that is not discovered immediately after the first day's use. Owing to the superb quality of our No. M Basket Ball, our customers have grown to expect a season's use of one ball, and at times make unreasonable claims under our guarantee, which we will not allow.

A. G. SPALDING & BROS.

No. ML

No. **ML.** Spalding **"Official Lined" Basket Ball.** Superior to any except our No. M Official Basket Ball. Case is made of best quality pebble grain leather, in four sections with capless ends. Guaranteed rubber bladder, lacing needle and rawhide lace. . . . . Each, **$12.00**

SPALDING BASKET BALLS

No. M2

SPALDING "SUPERIOR" BASKET BALL

No. M-2. Good quality pebble grain leather, eight section case, with guaranteed rubber bladder, needle and lace. . . . . . . Each, $11.00

SPALDING PRACTICE BASKET BALL

No. M3. Case of good weight durable leather. Guaranteed bladder, needle and lace. . . . . . Each, $7.50

SPALDING PLAYGROUND BASKET BALLS

No. PGO. Made of strong, pebbled leather. Specially protected seams for playground use. Regulation size. Guaranteed bladder, lacing needle and rawhide lace. . . Each, $12.00

No. PVO. "Army and Navy." Outseam style. Durable leather. Guaranteed bladder, lacing needle and lace. . . . . . . Each, $9.00

No. PKO. "Service." Outseam style. Good leather. Guaranteed bladder, lace and needle. . . . Each, $8.00

CANVAS BASKET BALL HOLDER

No. 01. Useful for teams to carry properly inflated basket ball. Each, $3.25

SPALDING BLADDERS

No. OM. For Nos. M, ML, M2, M3, PGO, PVO, PKO balls. Each, $1.15
No. A. Bladder. . . . " .90

SPALDING SCORE BOOKS

Each
No. 10. Paper cover, 10 games. . 20c.
No. 11. Cloth cover, 25 games. . 50c.
No. A. Collegiate, paper cover, 10 games. . . . . Each, 20c.
No. B. Collegiate, cloth cover, 25 games. . . . . Each, 50c.
No. N. For Women. . . " 50c.

Send for our Basket Ball Catalogue. Free on request.

No. M3

SPALDING BASKET BALL SUNDRIES

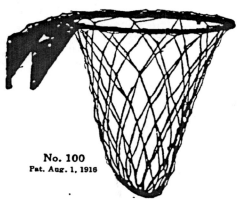

No. 100
Pat. Aug. 1, 1916

No. 100 Basket Ball Goals

The Spalding No. 100 goal—made under the Schommer patent, dated Aug. 1, 1916, No. 1,193,024—is the outcome of constant efforts to make a goal without the side braces, and yet rigid and firm enough to stand rough usage. It is made of a two-piece malleable iron bracket and a steel ring.

The elimination of the side braces does away with the hazard of hitting them in "close up shots"; of deflecting the ball at any angle, making the judge of the rebound a rank guess; of slowing up the game by the ball lodging between the braces and the back board; of stopping the game due to a broken side brace, and the shifting of the braces to all kinds of angles when they work loose. Bracket has a large bearing surface which gives far more rigidity and strength than the old types. Mathematically constructed so as to conform with the rules, and yet no ball thrown for the goal can be deflected by the bracket. Complete with nets. Pair, $10.00

No. 50. **Detachable.** Can be detached readily from wall or upright, leaving no obstruction to interfere with other games or gymnasium work. With nets. Pr., $10.00

No. 90. **Drop-Forged.** So far as we know this is the only drop-forged goal made. Practically unbreakable; with extra heavy nets. . . . . Pair, $10.00

No. 70. **Practice.** Substantial in construction. Complete with nets. " 7.50

Spalding Nets, Separate, for Goals

Made of heavy twine; hand knitted; white .. . . Pair, 85c.

Spalding Basket Ball Whistles

No. 4   No. 3   No. 7   No. 2

No. 4. Horn Whistle; nickel-plated, made of heavy metal. Each, $1.10
No. 3. Nickel-plated. . " .55
No. 2. Reliable; popular design. .30

No. 7. Nickel-plated, heavy metal whistle. . . . . . Each, 75c.
No. 7S. Same as No. 7, but with band for holding on two fingers. Ea., 75c.

No. AB

No. BBL

SPALDING SUCTION SOLE SHOES

No. AB. High Blucher cut, leather, heavy red rubber suction soles, superior quality. Pair, $8.50
No. BBL. Women's. High cut; light, black leather; good red rubber suction soles. " 8.25

No. P

No. PA

SPECIAL CANVAS TOP RUBBER SOLED SHOES

No. AC. High cut; canvas top, reinforced eyelets; special quality plain rubber soles. Pair, $4.50
No. P. Special quality soft rubber suction soles. Ventilating holes. Sizes 6½ to 12. " 3.50
    Sizes, 2½ to 6. " 3.25
No. PL. Women's. Otherwise similar to No. P. . . . . " 3.25
No. PA. Diamond suction design rubber soles. Lace down to toes. Sizes, 6½ to 12. " 4.00
    Sizes, 2½ to 6. " 3.75

HIGH GRADE CANVAS SHOES

Best grade white canvas uppers and rubber soles.

No. IH. High cut. Men's. Sizes, 6 to 12, inclusive. . . . . Pair, $2.50
No. I. Low cut. Men's. Sizes, 6 to 12, inclusive. . . . . " 2.25
No. IHB. High cut. Boys'. Sizes, 2½ to 5, inclusive. . . . . " 2.25
No. IB. Low cut. Boys'. Sizes, 2½ to 5, inclusive. . . . . " 2.00
No. IHX. High cut. Youths' Sizes, 11 to 2, inclusive. . . . . " 2.00
No. IX. Low cut. Youths'. Sizes, 11 to 2, inclusive. . . . . " 1.75

WOMEN'S AND MISSES' SIZES

No. IHL. High cut. Sizes, 2½ to 8, inclusive. . . . . Pair, $2.25
No. IHLX. High cut. Sizes, 11 to 2, inclusive. . . . . " 2.00

SPALDING

The Real Meaning of a Trade Mark

Some trade marks are merely symbols of a commercial enterprise and have no intrinsic value. They soon fade.

Other trade marks have a deeper significance. They are the visible sign of quality and their pre-eminence represents the accumulation of years of good will based upon honest workmanship and fair dealing.

The Spalding trade mark has earned its reputation in the latter class

This trade mark means much to you

It answers your question, "Why should I buy athletic goods of A. G. Spalding & Bros.?—or

What do I get for my money when I buy Spalding goods?

Like the Rock of Gibraltar, it does not talk, yet it stands for much—permanence and dependability.

The Spalding Trade Mark on any article of athletic equipment is a guarantee that the materials are the finest, the workmanship the best, the prices fair and the design as modern as nearly half a century of progressive development can make it.

It says to you—Spalding's Athletic Goods are the best. There are no better made.

A. G. Spalding & Bros

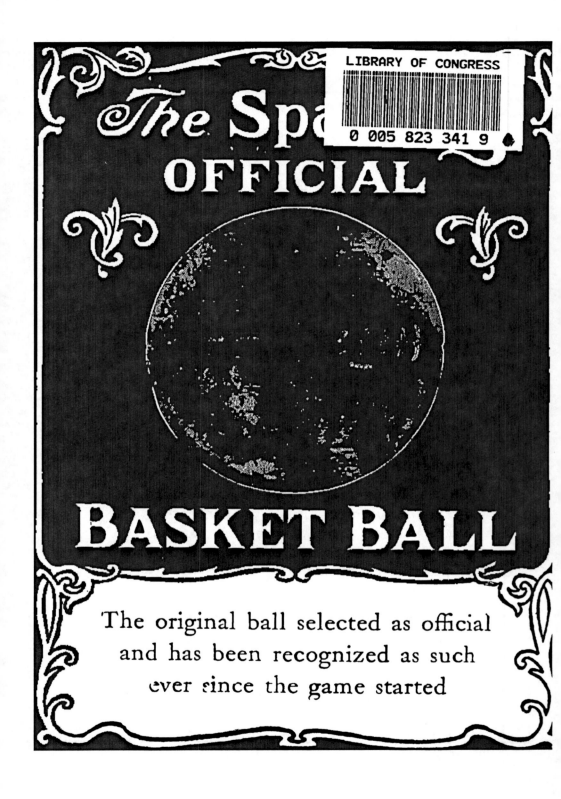

The Sp

OFFICIAL

BASKET BALL

The original ball selected as official
and has been recognized as such
ever since the game started

CPSIA information can be obtained at www.ICGtesting.com
Printed in the USA
LVOW09*1416091115

461709LV00003B/3/P

A day at Versailles

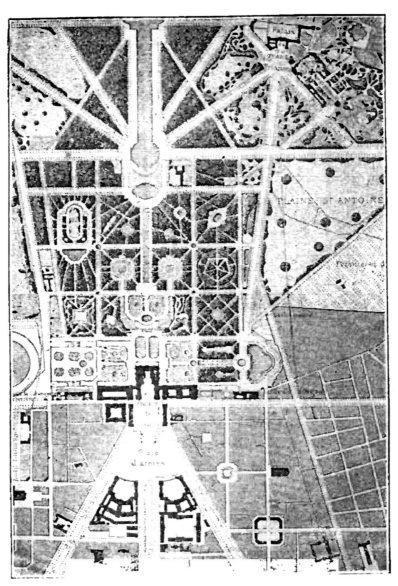

LEFT BANK RAILY   TRAMWAY   RIGHT BANK RAILY

FAME WRITING THE HISTORY OF LOUIS XIV

A DAY

VERSAILLES

ILLUSTRATED GUIDE
TO THE PALACE, MUSEUM, PARK
AND THE TRIANONS

WOOD-CUTS AND PLANS

G. BRAUN
ÉDITEUR OFFICIEL DES MUSÉES NATIONAUX
18, rue Louis-le-Grand, 18

1919

INTRODUCTION

Vast numbers of visitors come to Versailles to spend a
day in visiting the Palace, its halls and rooms, the Museum,
the Park, and the Trianons. It is advisable if possible to
divide the visit into two or three days, but it is possible in a
single day to see this fine collection, if no time be lost and the
visitor be well directed. Such is the object of the present
guide. In following exactly the routes we indicate, and in
examining those objects which are mentioned as worthy of
attention, and at the same time passing rapidly where we
recommend no stay to be made, the visitor will leave the
Palace having seen all its beauties : ceilings and decorations,
grand marble mosaics, sculptured and gilded wainscotting,
lintels, copper carvings, antique furniture, pictures, busts,
etc. That is to say the visitor will have had under his eyes
the most beautiful specimens of the xvii[th] and xviii[th] cen-

turies. The connoisseur, the casual visitor and the artist will all find their tastes gratified, whether of pleasure or utility.

A few historical notes will furnish all necessary information upon what has been done in the galleries and halls, and what purpose they served in times past, from what period they date, their style, and the principal artists whose master-pieces they are.

The engravings which accompany the text will assist the visitor in retaining a souvenir of what he may have admired. The plans will facilitate the inspection of the halls of the Palace, the principal rooms of the Museum, the gardens and statues of the Park.

For the visit to the Museum it has been thought unnecessary to give a complete list of the pictures, as each one bears a label indicating the subject and name of the artist. Those who may wish to possess full details will find them in the catalogue of Eudore Soulié in three volumes and a supplement, giving a description of the 5000 works of art contained in the museum. One may however consult with greater satisfaction the recent volume of Messrs Nolbac (curator of the Museum) and A. Pérate, entitled the *National Museum of Versailles*, and containing 110 reproductions of the principal works.

The object of the present guide is to give the public the satisfaction of seeing everything of interest, and carrying away a complete idea of that most admirable work of art, the Palace of Versailles.

The Villas of the Grand and Little Trianons complete Ver-

sailles. In order to have an exact idea of the residence of
the former monarchs, the visitor should not omit to visit these
two Villas of which the Little Trianon displays a most charm:·
ing example of the style of Louis XVI.

L. B.

HOW TO REACH VERSAILLES FROM PARIS

Versailles can be reached in about 35 minutes by railway
being 30 trains a day each way between the Saint-Lazare .
and 30 trains by Invalides Station Paris and Versailles, 29 .
from the Montparnasse Station. The fares are 1 fr. 65 first class,
1 fr. 15 second class, single journey, by Saint-Lazare Station, and
1 fr. 50 and 90 centimes by Montparnasse and Invalides stations.

The most enjoyable way, however, is by the four-in-hand carriages
of Messrs Cook, which leave their Office place de l'Opera in front of
the Grand Opera House every day. except Monday. The itinerary covered
by these carriage drives is as follows, and the fare 8 shillings.

ROUTE OF COOK'S CARRIAGE DRIVES

Church of St. Augustin, Parc Monceau, Arc de Triomphe, Bois de
Boulogne, Lakes, Grand Cascade. Racecourse of Longchamps, Citadel
of Mont Valérien, Town and Park of St. Cloud, Montretout-Buzenval.
Forest of Ville-d'Avray, Avenue de Picardie, Versailles, Grand Trianon,
Private Apartments of the Empress Josephine, Napoleon I., etc., and
State Carriages (time for luncheon). Palace, Museum and Park
of Versailles, Avenue de Paris, Viroflay, Chaville, Sèvres, Porcelain
Manufactory, Billancourt, Fortifications of Paris, Viaduct of Auteuil,
Palace and Park of the Trocadéro, Embankment of the Seine, Cours
la Reine.

Cook's Four-in-Hand Excursions start at ten o'clock precisely, returning at half past five, in time for table d'hôte dinner. Tickets
should be secured on the previous day

wha
they
pieces

A DAY

AT

VERSAILLES

I

HISTORICAL

The Palace of Versailles is one of the most perfect buildings in France from an artistic point of view, and certainly the most instructive for visitors. It was built in its original form under Louis XIII, enlarged by Louis XIV to its present immense size, and inhabited by the French kings up to the Revolution. It has since been converted into a museum and, having continued to play a part in great national events, presents to the public a collection of the most interesting souvenirs of France.

The history of the Palace is markedly shown in its construction. Standing in the entrance court, on the spot where the modern statue of Louis XIV is placed, and where formerly stood the entrance of the railing forming the royal court between the two wings of the Palace, we notice buildings of different periods.

A portion of the brick and stone constructions growing narrower towards the elegant marble court, under the windows of Louis XIV room, dates from Louis XIII.

Louis XIII was in reality the true founder of Versailles and (his architect was probably Le Roy) built there in 1624 a hunting box of which something is preserved amidst the gorgeous buildings of Louis XIV.

This little box of Louis XIII was little to speak of. It formed only the three sides of the narrow called *cour de marbre* (marble court), the pavement of which as well as the central façade and the decoration of the roof date from Louis XIV.

All the portions of the Chateau, of the court and the forecourt, where again brick predominates, belong to the first enlargements of the Chateau by Louis XIV, who firstly adopted the hunting box of his father as a rendez-vous of pleasure and gave there a series of court festivities still celebrated. The wings acquired the name of *Ailes des Ministres* in 1682, at the time of the installation of the offices of the government, when the Grand King settled at Versailles and established there the seat of Royalty.

The work of Louis XIV is very noticeable on the side of the Palace towards the gardens. But on the entrance side our attention is arrested by a building of Louis XV's time, a massive heavy-looking wing, called after its designer " the Gabriel wing ". It was built in the year 1772, and formed part of a plan for the entire remodelling of the Palace. In accordance with the taste of the hour, the idea was to rebuild the entire centre in Greco-Roman style.

This grievous work of vandalism was interrupted by the financial distress of the country under Louis XVI. Napoléon I intended to resume it, and ordered Dufour to begin the companion wing to that of Louis XV of which the Pavilion only was completed in 1820. The Gabriel wing and the Dufour Pavilion occupy the place of colonnaded pavilions of the time of Louis XIV which we see in old pictures and against which abutted the railing enclosing the Royal Court.

The endless façade on the gardens gives the most just idea of the extent of the Chateau and the immense work of Louis XIV, the size of which it is impossible to take in at a single glace from the parterre.

The main body of the Chateau completely covering the small square original building is the work of the architect Le Vau: the large wings that of Mansart. But the front façade of the Chateau underwent a considerable change in 1679. The central portion of the first storey of Le Vau's building consisted of a large terrace at the two extremities of which was a large salon.

This change dates from 1679. The main building of the Palace is older by ten years, and the great wings on the south and north were begun, one in 1679, and the other in 1684. The Chapel, surmounted by its gilded lantern, was built between 1699 and 1710. All then that we see of the Palace from the grounds dates from the reign of Louis XIV. The visitor will be interested in the old pictures in room 54 of the Museum, showing the different enlargements of the Palace.

The different periods of architecture are as clearly shown in the interior as on the exterior. Nowhere may the three great decorative styles of the xvii[th] and xviii[th] centuries be studied from more perfect or more correctly dated models.

In spite of restorations and mutilations, the ancient works of art collected at Versailles are, as a whole, second to none in France. It is indeed the Museum of National Decorative Art, which would be easy to complete by the addition of some fine pieces of furniture, so as to recall what was formerly there.

The day of the Revolution, October 6th 1789, recalled Louis XVI to Paris, and withdrew the seat of government from

Versailles. The Revolution did not harm the Palace, but the Convention ordered all the furniture to be sold, thus scattering treasures which are now almost priceless. The Directoire established there an ephemeral Museum of the French school. Napoléon and afterwards Louis XVIII intended living at the Palace.

The final destiny of the Palace was fixed by Louis-Philippe, who appropriated to it enormous sums from the civil list, and made a great Museum, consecrated " to All the Glories of France ". This Museum, inaugurated in 1837, has in reality become a museum of French history under all its aspects, and its collections are the most important and numerous of those of the same kind in Europe.

We cannot help regretting that the creation of new galleries has led to the destruction of several fine suites of rooms, and the decorative treasures they contained. But it has probably preserved the Palace to the Nation, by giving it a worthy use ; and the number of works of art — both paintings and statuary — which is collected there, is precious to history and art.

A general rearrangement of the Museum, particularly in the portrait galleries, has recently been undertaken, and has already given satisfaction to the public. The resources placed in the hands of the administration are unfortunately insufficient. The Museum only contains works of an historic character. Everywhere accurate descriptions assist the observations of visitors.

Fresh acquisitions, some presented, others purchased by the State of the contemporaneous portion are constantly flowing in to fill up existing deficiencies.

The National Museum only occupies the centre of the Palace and a portion of the wings. The rest has been under the jurisdiction of Parliament since the National Assembly placed the seat of Government at Versailles in 1871. The hall to

THE PALACE OF VERSAILLES

which the Museum was then confined (formerly the opera house) became in 1875 the Senate house, and there was built at this time a hall for the Chamber of Deputies, to-day in use as the Hall of Congress.

.*.

Briefly the chief historical events of which the Palace of Versailles has been the scene are as follows :

Louis XIV (the Grand Monarch) died here 1715.
Louis XV died 1775. Here also Damiens tried to assassinate him.
Louis XVI, who was guillotined Jan. 21, 1793, was forcibly carried away from the Palace of Versailles in 1789.
In 1793 the Palace was converted into a manufactory of arms, and in 1815 it was pillaged by the Prussians.
After the fall of Napoléon it was occupied in succession by Louis XVIII, Charles X and Louis-Philippe.
In 1855 Queen Victoria was received here by Napoléon III.
In 1871 the Palace was occupied by the German forces and on the 18th of January King William of Prussia was here proclaimed Emperor of Germany.
After the departure of the German troops it became the seat of the Government of France under the presidency of M. Thiers and continued so until the year 1880, when the Government was removed to Paris.

THE MARBLE COURT

II

THE PALACE AND THE MUSEUM.

THE PARADE GROUND.

The Palace is built on a hill, and is faced by a large square, known as the " Place d'armes " or " Parade ", which unites three large avenues — in the centre the Paris avenue, to the right that of Saint-Cloud, and to the left that of Sceaux. The whole has a majestic appearance which prepares us for the contemplation of the magnificent residence of Louis XIV.

The avenue of Saint-Cloud is separated from that of Paris by the " Great Stables ", where the king's horses used to be kept, and the avenues of Paris and Sceaux are separated by a similar structure, the " Little Stables ", where the carriages were kept. To-day, one contains artillery workshops, and the other Barracks of Engineers.

The two stables were designed by Mansart, and have contained as many as 2500 horses.

THE COURTS OF THE PALACE.

The entrance-court, or avant-cour, is separated from the Place d'armes by a long iron-railing with three gilded bays. The centre one is surmonted by an escutcheon with the arms of France, a master piece of iron-work.

This court lies between the two great buildings called

XTERIOR OF THE CHAPEL

" w.ngs of the ministers ", where the ministers of the old monarchy lived, and where several ministries took refuge in the Commune of 1871.

The sixteen marble statues in the court, which are 4 mètres (13 feet) high, were placed there by Louis-Philippe, at the time of the conversion of the Palace into a museum. With the exception of those of four marshals of the Empire, they were executed in the time of Louis XVIII for the decoration of the bridge of Concord, Paris.

The equestrian statue of Louis XIV, executed in bronze by order of Louis-Philippe, marks the entrance to the Court Royal, which was formerly separated from the fore-court by an iron-railing. The part between the buildings built nearest together is called the marble court; its marble flags have recently been restored.

We can enter the Chateau on the left by the grand staircase known as « The Queen's Stairs », which opens on the Court Royal. But it is preferable to make our way at once to the right, towards the little Chapel-Court, where we find the principal entrance to the museum.

THE CHAPEL.

We notice the upper cornice of the Chapel, which is one of the most beautiful portions of the architecture of the Palace, with its stone statues and windows ornamented with elegant sculptures. The Chapel was built between 1699 and 1710 by Mansart and his successor Robert de Cotte.

If we intend examining in detail the interior of the Chapel we must speak to the officer at the entrance to the museum, but we can study it at leisure up the first floor, the doors being always open.

The principal entrance to the museum is at the end of the Chapel Court, under the passage to the right.

INTERIOR OF THE CHAPEL

ENTRANCE TO THE MUSEUM

If we are pressed for time, we must, on entering, turn to the right, past the large bas-relief (Passage of the Rhine by Louis XIV) and enter the "African Rooms" by the door into the Stone Gallery (Smalah, etc., page 26). If we only wish to see the state-apartments, we must ascend the staircase by the side of the chapel-door, which leads to the upper vestibule (page 30).

If we have plenty of time, or the chance of coming again, we will enter by the door to the left of the bas-relief, where the stall of books and photographs stands. This brings us to the

FIRST ROOMS OF FRENCH HISTORY (2 to 11).

These rooms contain pictures recalling the principal historic deeds from the time of Clovis up to the Revolution. The visitor will find the works of such modern artists as Paul Delaroche (*Charlemagne crossing the Alps*), Ary Scheffer (*The death of Gaston de Foix*), Schnetz, Larivière, Cabanel, etc. Among the pictures of the time of Louis XIV and Louis XV, are to be found the works of Van der Meulen, Testelin, the two Martins, Parrocel, etc. Each picture bears an explanatory label.

Going out at the bottom of the staircase built in 1851 and turning to the right is the

STONE GALLERY (16).

This contains chiefly pieces of sculpture of the middle ages (casts of the royal statues on the tombs of St. Denis, or marbles executed after these statues). In the centre is the tomb of Ferdinand, King of Aragon, and Isabella, Queen of Castile, a great cast taken from the marble original at Granada.

THE STONE GALLERY

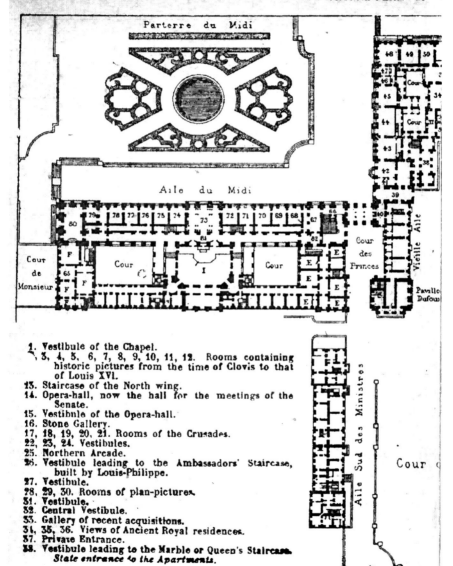

1. Vestibule of the Chapel.
, 3, 4, 5, 6, 7, 8, 9, 10, 11, 12. Rooms containing
   historic pictures from the time of Clovis to that
   of Louis XVI.
13. Staircase of the North wing.
14. Opera-hall, now the hall for the meetings of the
   Senate.
15. Vestibule of the Opera-hall.
16. Stone Gallery.
17, 18, 19, 20, 21. Rooms of the Crusades.
22, 23, 24. Vestibules.
25. Northern Arcade.
26. Vestibule leading to the Ambassadors' Staircase,
   built by Louis-Philippe.
27. Vestibule.
28, 29, 30. Rooms of plan-pictures.
31. Vestibule.
32. Central Vestibule.
33. Gallery of recent acquisitions.
34, 35, 36. Views of Ancient Royal residences.
37. Private Entrance.
38. Vestibule leading to the Marble or Queen's Staircase.
   State entrance to the Apartments.

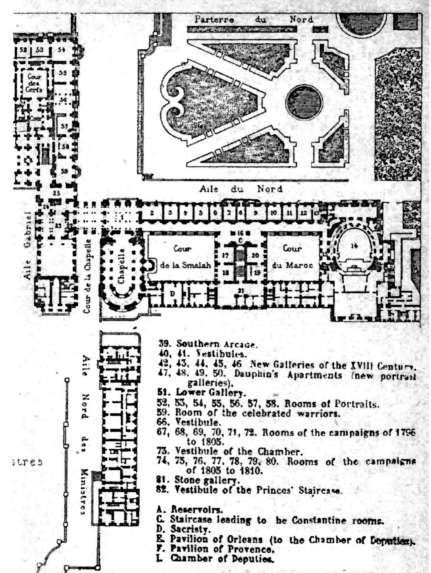

39. Southern Arcade.
40, 41. Vestibules.
42, 43, 44, 45, 46. New Galleries of the XVIII Century.
47, 48, 49, 50. Dauphin's Apartments (new portrait galleries).
51. Lower Gallery.
52, 53, 54, 55, 56, 57, 58. Rooms of Portraits.
59. Room of the celebrated warriors.
66. Vestibule.
67, 68, 69, 70, 71, 72. Rooms of the campaigns of 1796 to 1805.
73. Vestibule of the Chamber.
74, 75, 76, 77, 78, 79, 80. Rooms of the campaigns of 1805 to 1810.
81. Stone gallery.
82. Vestibule of the Princes' Staircase.

A. Reservoirs.
C. Staircase leading to the Constantine rooms.
D. Sacristy.
E. Pavilion of Orleans (to the Chamber of Deputies).
F. Pavilion of Provence.
L. Chamber of Deputies.

On the right is the entrance to the

ROOMS OF THE CRUSADES (17-21).

The pictures in these rooms commemorate the history of the expeditions in the East between the 11th and 13th centuries, made by Christian Europe for the deliverance of Jerusalem and the Holy Sepulchre. The ceilings, friezes and pillars bear armour belonging to kings, princes and knights, who took part in the Crusades.

The doors of cedar-wood and the bronze mortar placed in the largest room come from the hospital of the Knights of Rhodes.

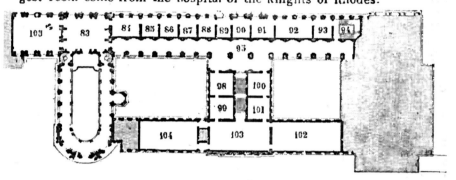

RIGHT WING, 1st FLOOR

On leaving the rooms of the Crusades, the visitor should ascend the staircase marked *Africa, Crimea, Italy*, and enter the large

ROOM OF CONSTANTINE (103).

On the end wall are three great pictures by Horace Vernet, representing the capture of Constantine. The picture on the left, the *Assault*, is probably the finest work. The other paintings in the room are also by Horace Vernet. All the figures of officers and soldiers are from portraits. We enter on the right

THE SMALAH ROOM (104).

The celebrated picture by H. Vernet (69 1/2 by nearly 16 ft) represents the *Taking of the Smalah* from Abd-el-Kader by the Duke d'Aumale in 1845.

CONSTANTINE ROOM

On the right is the *Battle of Isly*, gained by marshal Bugeaud over the Moors in 1844; and opposite, the *Siege of Rome* and episodes from the Mexican war.

In a cabinet is a bas-relief by Carpeaux, *Napoleon III receiving Abd-el-Kader*, and an English clock taken in 1830 from the Dey of Algiers.

Re-crossing the Constantine Room we come to the

CRIMEAN AND ITALIAN ROOM.

This contains complete illustrations of the expedition in the Crimea, notably the fine painting by Pils (*Battle of Alma*) and the three pictures by Yvon illustrating the *Capture of the Malakoff* (1855). There are also watercolours on the Siege of Sebastopol, and busts of generals who took part in the campaign.

The Italian war (1859) is represented by two pictures by Yvon : *Magenta* and *Solferino*.

From the Constantine Room visitors can enter the Stone Gallery on the first floor, situated immediately above that on the ground-floor, by two passages, each formed of two rooms filled with interesting modern pictures. Either passage will serve.

MODERN ROOMS (99 to 101).

In the rooms on the left the visitor will notice *the Retreat from Russia, the Battle of Inkermann*, by Gustave Doré, *the Reception of Siamese Ambassadors at Fontainebleau*, by Gérôme, etc.

In the rooms on the right : — *The Federation Fête in* 1790, by Couder, *the Volunteers of* 1792, by Vinchon, *the Last Victims of the Terror*, by Muller, *the Meeting of Napoleon and Czar Alexander*, by Serangeli, etc.

After visiting this modern part of the *Museum, visitors pressed for time should turn to the left into the sculpture gallery, and go direct to the Chapel Vestibule (page 30).

Others should turn to the right arriving at the grand staircase at the extremity of the wing, and ascend to the second storey to see the important collection of *historical portraits* exhibited in the

NORTH ATTIC (galleries 153-162).

Visitors should enter by the door near the windows. The first room is reserved exclusively for the xvi[th] century, and contains some valuable portraits on wood of princes, ladies and historical personages. The oldest work (xv[th] century) represents Joan of Arc in armour, on the left of the Virgin, on whose right is St. Michael·

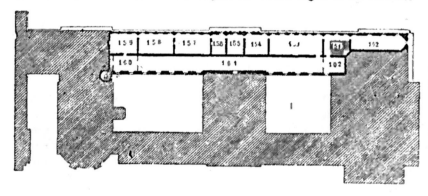

THE NORTH ATTIC

the features are no longer discernible, but the heroine carries a cloud of sanctity which bears witness to the veneration with which the people of her time regarded the liberator of France.

Chronological order is maintained in the following rooms and the gallery, which present most instructive illustrations of French history in the shape of portraits of famous characters. The series of Louis XIV's time, thanks to Beaubrun, Lefèvre, Bourdon, Mignard, Le Brun, Nocret, Rigaud, are particularly rich in fine pictures. These rooms are being re-arranged with a view to showing the paintings to a better advantage.

The gallery is dedicated to the reigns of Louis XV and Louis XVI, and contains portraits by Rigaud, Largillière, Vanloo, Tocqué, Drouais, Mme Labille-Guiard, Mme Vigée-Lebrun, etc.

Ascending the staircase, we re-enter the

ROOMS OF FRENCH HISTORY (93-84).

The first room is filled with souvenirs of
the reign of Louis-Philippe, the second and
third with those of the Restoration; the
others follow the course of French History
up to the time of the Egyptian Expedition.
The visitor will notice many military pie-

tures of the First Empire, which are all of
great historical interest.

Next comes the

CHAPEL VESTIBULE (83).

The construction is of the same period
as the chapel (late Louis XIV). The king
used to enter the Tribune through this vestibule. The visitor
is now in a good position for inspecting the upper part of the
Chapel, and the paintings of the voulted roof.

CHAPEL VESTIBULE

These paintings represent : — In the Centre, *the Eternal Father in all his Glory*, by Coypel ; at the end, *the Resurrection*, by Delafosse ; above the King's Tribune, *the Descent of the Holy Spirit*, by Jouvenet.

The high altar is surmounted by a *Celestial Glory* in gilded bronze, by Van Clève.   The pillars and all surfaces are decorated with magnificent bas-reliefs.

The visitor should notice the gilded sculptures of the door leading to the Tribune, and the beautiful lock of wrought copper.

At the side is

THE ROOM OF HERCULES (105)

This was the great court ball-room of the xviii century.   It only dates from the beginning of the reign of Louis XV. The ceiling, one of the largest in existence (59 × 55 ft), represents the *Apotheosis of Hercules*.

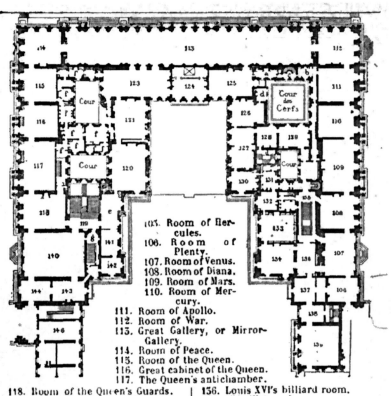

105. Room of Hercules.
106. Room of Plenty.
107. Room of Venus.
108. Room of Diana.
109. Room of Mars.
110. Room of Mercury.
111. Room of Apollo.
112. Room of War.
113. Great Gallery, or Mirror-Gallery.
114. Room of Peace.
115. Room of the Queen.
116. Great cabinet of the Queen.
117. The Queen's antichamber.

118. Room of the Queen's Guards.
119. Queen's (or marble) Staircase.
120. Room of the King's Guards.
121. King's Antichamber.
123. Room with oval-window (Ox-eye room).
124. Louis XIV's room.
125. Chamber of the King or Council.
126. Louis XV's room.
127. Clock room.
128. Antechamber of the dogs.
129. Louis XV's dining-hall.
130. Louis XV cabinet.
131. Second cabinet of Louis XV.
132. Cabinet of Madame Adélaïde.
133. Louis XVI's library.
134. Porcelain room.
135. Ambassadors' Staircase (built uis-Philippe).

136. Louis XVI's billiard room.
137. 138. Watercolour-room.
139. Room of the States-General.
140. Great Guard-Room.
141, 142, 143, 144, Historical rooms from 1792 to 1796.
146. Watercolour-room.

a. Bath-room.
b. Room of wigs.
c. Landing on the Staircase of the Furnace.
d. Room in Louis XVI style.
e. Vestibule of the Queen's Staircase.
f. Rooms of Marie-Antoinette.
g. Stucco staircase, leading to the Attic of Chimay

3

This fine work-of-art, painted on prepared canvas, was finished by Lemoine in 1736, and cleverly restored in 1885.

The magnificent decorative bronzes in this room are by Vassé. The visitor should notice those of the fire-place, and the border of the picture representing *the Passage of the Rhine* in 1672.

The door leads to the State apartments of Louis XIV.

ROOM OF PLENTY (106).

The ceiling, painted by Rouasse, represents " Plenty " or "Royal Magnificence ". There are some large pieces of handiwork in gold and some agate vases which represent the furniture of the Palace. The pictures, replacing ancient tapestries, are by Van der Meulen, the principal painter of battle scenes in Louis XIV's time.

The visitor, before further examining these apartments, can visit some of the smaller rooms, entering by the door opposite the window.

THE WATERCOLOUR ROOMS (137, 138).

Here are some valuable watercolours by Van Blarenberghe, relating to the campaigns of Louis XV, and remarkable for the number of small figures and the accuracy of the details of the landscape. There are also : — Costumes of Infantry under Louis XV, Views of the gardens of Versailles, etc.

ROOM OF THE STATES-GENERAL (139).

The frieze of this room represents the procession on the eve of the reunion of the States-General in 1789, at Versailles. The picture by Couder represents the opening of the States-Council by Louis XVI, in the room of Pocket-Money (Menus Plaisirs), Street of Workshops.

There are two great pictures recalling the war of 1870-71 : *Charge of the Cuirassiers at Morsbronn* (battle of Reichshoffen), by Aimé Morot, and the *Fight of the Plâtrière* (battle of Champigny), by Alphonse de Neuville.

Re-entering the Room of Plenty and the Grand Apartments, we come to the

ROOM OF VENUS (107).

The five rooms of which this
is the first, each bear the name
of a planet, and the presiding
divinity is represented on the
ceiling with his or her principal
attributes. The fine carving of the
doors, the work of Caffieri, give
the different emblems belonging
to each name. The visitor should
notice the figure of Louis XIV and
his personal emblem, the Sun.
The locks, equally remarkable,
the door-handles, and the win-
dow-sashes, are the work of the
Italian carver, Dominique Cucci.

The Grand Apartments were
sumptuously furnished, and hung
with Gobelin tapestry representing the history of Louis XIV.
These rooms were used three
times a week for the celebrated
receptions of the Court, which
was for the most part confined
to the great wings of the Palace.
Some were set apart for games,
others for music and dancing.
The room of Venus was the re-
freshment room. In the niche
is a statue of Louis XIV as a Roman
Emperor.

At the right there was formerly a door opening on the great

Ambassadors' Staircase, a master-piece of architecture, destroyed in the overhauling of the Palace in the time of Louis XV.

The whole room is lined with most beautiful marble mosaics; so perfect is their construction that none have been displaced for more than two centuries. Above the door are some bas-reliefs in gilded copper.

ROOM OF DIANA (108).

The room of Diana was, in the time of Louis XIV, the billiard-room. The ceiling represents Diana presiding over Navigation and the Chase. The decoration of the room, like that of the preceding one, is exactly as it was in Louis XIV's time. There is a table topped with Florence mosaics, which is one of the rarest pieces of furniture of the time. It was brought to Versailles at the time of its conversion into a Museum.

Opposite the windows is a bust of the King by the sculptor Bernin, the most celebrated Italian artist of that time.

ROOM OF MARS (109).

The ceiling represents the God of War in a car drawn by wolves.

Over the fireplace is a picture of Louis XIV as a child on horseback, with the bridge of Pont-Neuf in the back-ground. This room like the following, was hung with magnificent tapestry. The celebrated compositions of the history of the king, by Le Brun and Van der Meulen were woven for them at the Goblins.

Some of these hangings have been recently replaced. Those of the room represent the *Taking of Dôle* and the *Entrance of the King at Dunkirk.*

ROOM OF MERCURY (110).

On the ceiling, Mercury drawn in a car by two cocks, is

accompanied by Vigilance. The room was used in the time
of Louis XIV as a state-chamber, and had a bed with a balustrade of wrought silver in front.

The tapestry (de haute lisse) represents the Siege of Tour-

DESIGN ON THE ARCH OF CEILING

nai, Louis XIV at the siege of Douai and the Defeat of the
Spaniards near Bruges.

ROOM OF APOLLO (111).

This was the throne-room, and in it Louis XIV gave audience to ambassadors.

The beautiful ceiling painted by Lafosse, represents Apollo (to whom the Sun-King is so often compared) on his car accompanied by the Seasons.

The tapestry represents the *Interview of Louis XIV and Philip IV*, the *Marriage of the King and Infante Marie-Thérèse* and the *Audience to the ambassador of Spain*.

ROOM OF WAR (112).

This room is a companion to the Glass-Gallery and Room of Peace, at the other extremity. The three ceilings were painted by Charles Le Brun, first painter to the King, and designer of all the decoration of the Palace.

All the ornaments of the Room of War, trophies and bas-reliefs, are consistent with its name. The ceiling represents France surrounded by the victories of Louis XIV; on the arched vaults are four symbolical pictures, Bellona in fury (opposite the fire-place), Holland, Germany and Spain.

The bas-relief in stucco, *Louis XIV on horseback*, is the work of Coysevox, one of the greatest sculptors of the age.

The great trophies in gilded bronze in this room and the gallery were partly modelled by him; they are incomparable master-pieces.

Round the room are six busts of Roman Emperors, with heads of porphyry and marble draperies.

GREAT GALLERY, OR GLASS-GALLERY (113).

Louis XIV had this gallery built by Mansart over a terrace forming an alcove between two pavilions built by Levau. The decoration was directly superintended by Le Brun, who painted on the ceiling, in thirty scenes, the history of Louis XIV between 1662 and 1678. Each picture is enclosed in a sculptured border, richly gilt.

The explanatory inscriptions were made by Boileau and Racine An original sketch by Le Brun, *the Conquest of*

ROOM OF PEACE

Franche-Comté, placed on an easel, may be compared with the finished composition.

This Gallery is 244 feet long, 34 feet broad, and 42 feet high. Each of the 17 windows overlooking the gardens has a corresponding arch decorated with mirrors, joined with wrought copper. The great trophies of gilt copper affixed to magnificent marbles, and the 24 groups of children in the cornice, are models by the best sculptors of the time of Louis XIV.

This splendid decoration must have produced a striking effect·when the wonderful furniture of olden times filled the Gallery.

In Louis XIV's time it possessed two immense carpets of the Savonnerie, curtains of white damask, brocaded with gold, sconces, high-stands, chandeliers, consoles, stools and silver-boxes holding orange-trees, bowls and vases fashioned by the most skilled workmen. All these grand pieces of silver-ware disappeared about 1689, and were taken to the Mint to be re-cast.

They are shown in some of the pictures in the great apartments. They were replaced by some gilt furniture scarcely less magnificent than the former marvels, which was scattered in the same way as the rest of the furniture of Versailles, by the Revolutionary sale.

The most important Court fêtes took place in the Glass Gallery. Among modern events we should recall the Pontifical Benediction given from the balcony by Pope Pius VII, January 3rd, 1804; the Banquet inaugurating the Museum, in 1837; the Fête in honour of the Queen of England, 1855; the Coronation of the king of Prussia, as Emperor of Germany, January 18th, 1871 ; the Ball given by Marshal Mac-Mahon, at the close of the Universal Exhibition of 1878; the solemn cele-,bration of the Centenary of the States-General by President Carnot and all the ministers of State, May 5th, 1889 ; and lastly.

THE GLASS-GALLERY

October 8ᵗʰ 1896, the reception of the Tzar, Nicholas II, who appeared on the balcony in view of the immense crowd gathered in front of the Palace.

The visitor should stand at one of the central windows and admire the symmetrical view of the gardens; close to the Palace is the reservoir with its two basins surrounded with bronze statues; then, in the distance, the lawn leading to the Grand-Canal, in the back-ground.

ROOM OF THE KING, OR COUNCIL (125).

The glass door on the first tier of the Gallery gives access to the Room of the King.

This hall dates from the second half of the reign of Louis XV. It was decorated in 1755 by the sculptor Antoine Rousseau. The visitor will notice the two large panels on either side of the fire-place, the bronzes of the fire-place, the bureau of Louis XV, the clock made in 1706, etc.

In Louis XIV's time this room was divided into two portions; the King's study occupied the part near his bed-chamber, and the end opening on to the Gallery formed the Room of Wigs, which used to hold the wigs that the King changed several times a day.

The King used to hold his Council in this room, and work with one of his ministers several hours daily. Here were decided the most important state affairs of the 18ᵗʰ century. In this room took place the ceremony of " presentation " of the ladies newly admitted to the Court.

ROOMS OF LOUIS XV.

These *smaller apartments* (closed on the days when the Great Fountains play) may be visited under the conduct of an official. They were made at different periods of Louis XV's time in order to give the king more privacy. They served the same purpose under Louis XVI, and were richly re-furnished for the few hours the Emperor and Empress of Russia spent in them, October 8ᵗʰ, 1896.

ROOM OF THE KING OR COUNCIL

They are admirable specimens of the elegant style of Louis XV, and some pieces of furniture of the same time, unfortunately very rare, have been replaced here. Nearly all the wainscoting is by the sculptor Verberckt.

The first room is the *bed-chamber of Louis XV*, made in 1738 in place of a chief billiard-room of Louis XV. Louis XV died of small-pox here, on May 10th, 1774. Here the royal family met on the morning of October 6th 1789, when the Palace was invaded by the mob; and here Marie Antoinette passed long hours watching from the window the crowd that clamoured for her head.

The *clock-room* is so called after beautiful Passemant' clock, placed here in 1749, a masterpiece of mechanism, showing days, months, years, phases of the moon, etc. The case of wrought bronze, remarkable in itself, bears the signature of Jacques Cafueri. The copper meridian fixed in woodwork, enables the time-piece to be regulated.

The tables, in stucco, give plans of the principal royal hunts. The statuette is a model of the monument of Louis XV by Bouchardon. The lintels of the door were placed there in the present century. The visitor will notice the beauty of the frames of the looking-glasses, the carved panels, and the frieze of the ceiling.

The King's private study is probably the finest relic of Louis XV, and all the details are to be admired. It was from the window of this room that Louis XV, alone with a friend, watched the funeral procession of Madame de Pompadour, and uttered these words: " This is the last mark of respect I can show to her. " Here Louis XVI ordered Cardinal de Rohan, implicated in the Collier affair to appear before himself and the Queen, before his arrest in the Glass Gallery.

The furniture, which belongs to a back cabinet was arranged by Louis XV on the site of the Little Gallery of Louis XIV and the Ambassadors' Staircase which were destroyed in order to make an apartment for Madame Adelaïde communicating with that of the king her father.

At the present time there is here a rich hall called the *Music Room*, on account of the trophies in its decoration; this was the reception-room of the princess. There is also a *Library* made for Louis XVI in place of Madame Adelaïde's bedroom, and the King's private dining-room, made in 1770, called the Porcelain Room, because on the

1ᵐ of January the productions of the royal manufactury at Sèvres used to be displayed here.

LOUIS XV's STUDY

MADAME ADELAIDE'S ROOM

LOUIS XIV'S ROOM (124).

From the King's or Council-Room the visitor enters the central portion of the Palace, which was, from the year 1701, the bedroom of Louis XIV. Formerly it was used as the King's Study, and the bedroom was in the neighbouring portion (Oval Window). In this bedroom there took place each day a solemn and complicated function — the King's toilet. He used to dine " au petit couvert ", that is to say alone in his room, at a little square table in front of the middle window. The great audiences were given here; here, too, the King received the remonstrances of Parliament, seated in his armchair before the fire.

Louis XIV died here, September 1ᵐˡ 1715, after a reign of 72 years. Louis XV slept here till 1738. On the 6ᵗʰ of October 1789, Louis XVI and Marie-Antoinette were obliged to appear on the balcony before the Parisian mob which invaded the Palace and to promise that they would in future live at the Tuileries.

The decoration, in a fine style of Louis XIV's time, is all very old, as is the balustrade, which no one is allowed pass. Over the King's bed N. Coustou has represented France watching over the monarchy, between two seated figures. The ceiling was intended to be decorated with paintings, but these have never been executed.

The furniture does not strictly belong to the room. The different articles were collected, and the bed constructed, in the time of Louis-Philippe. The bed and arm-chairs were recovered with pieces of tapestry from the old furniture of the room of Apollo (111). The lace counterpane belonged to the bed of Maria-Theresa, who died in 1685.

Two objects of art should be particularly noted : the marble bust of the duchess of Burgundy, by Covsevox, and the wax

medallion of Louis XIV, taken in his 69ᵗʰ year. The medallion is finished with one of the King's own wigs.

ANTE-ROOM, OR OX-EYE ROOM (123).

The room derives its name from the oval window, so noticeable on entering, and is the celebrated Œil de Bœuf of
Carlyles "French Revolution". The high frieze represents a
children's hunt, and is one of the most beautiful decorative
works of Louis XIV's time. Remarkable over the fireplace is the
most magnificent bust of Louis XIV executed by Coysevox in 1681,
during the most brilliant period of this monarch's reign. Amongst
the pictures on wood is a large canvas by Nocret, representing
Louis XIV and his family as the gods and goddesses of Olympia
and which is an example of the sort of idolatry at the Court of
the Grand King.

There were formerly two different rooms here, one the bed-
chamber and the other the ante-room. After its reconstruc-
tion in 1701, the Ox-eye Room served as ante-chamber to the
King's room. The courtiers used to wait here at the audience-
time; it was thronged when the King held receptions. and
even when he rose in the morning and retired at night. It
was in the heart of the Court, and was reached from the
interior by the Glass Gallery (page 38).

The room is reached from without by the salon on the left (121),
which has two doors, and was the hall " du grand couvert ", that
is to say, the one where the king dined in public, and by the Guard
Room (120) opening on to the great marble staircase, which we
shall come upon again later on. Pictures of the XVIIᵗʰ century, notably some by Van der Meulen, adorn the two rooms.

In the Ox-eye Room there is one of the entrances to the Queen's
apartments (closed on the days when the great fountains play) to
which the visitor should have a guide. The entrance is sometimes
here and sometimes by the Queen's bed-chamber (page 53).

LOUIS XIV'S ROOM

4

ROOMS OF MARIE-ANTOINETTE.

(*f* in the plan.)

The suite of small rooms bearing this name, formerly off-shoots of the large apartment of the Queen, was entirely refitted for Marie-Antoinette. They had previously been occupied in a different form by Marie Leczinska, wife of Louis XV.

These rooms contain elegant models of the Louis XVI style.

The visitor will observe :

A passage communicating with the bed-chamber, by which Marie-Antoinette fled to the Ox-eye Room, to take refuge in Louis XVI's apartments from the mob which invaded her own on the memorable 6ᵗʰ of October.

The " Meridienne ", an octagonal cabinet with mirrored recess ornamented with copper, wrought and gilded by Forestier, bolts and door-handles with the monogram of Marie-Antoinette.

The Library, made for Marie-Antoinette, with the Austrian eagle on the drawer-handles.

The Second Library, containing a little chest of taffeta, adorned with charming miniatures, presented to the Queen on the birth of the first dauphin, who died in 1789, the elder brother of Louis XVII.

The Salon or large interior room, with a bust of Marie-Antoinette as a girl, by Pajow The furniture is Louis XVI style. The Sèvres time-piece belonged to the Queen. There is an absurd legend connected with the mirrors, which says that Marie-Antoinette was horrified at beholding herself without a head, when she came to Versailles. The mirrors were not in existence at the time, and the effect produced is common to all the mirrors of this kind (for example those in the " Meridienne ").

" The decoration is always white or gold, but very rich. The panels represent winged monsters leaning on smoking trivets, entwined with roses. Opposite the mirror which separates the windows is a glass niche, larger than that of the " Meridienne ", with the arch draped in silk. Charming furniture ornamented this recess, where Marie-Antoinette passed the greater part of her time. Her private audiences were given here; Gluck, Grétry, and the musicians she patronized, performed their music in this little room.

large enough for the entourage of a queen. " (P de Nolhac, *The reign of Marie-Antoinette*, p. 173.)

The bath-room, stripped of its furniture, is lighted like the other

THE ROOM OF MARIE-ANTOINETTE

rooms from small dull courtyards. At the side is a little sitting room with modern hangings.

The exit is through the Room of the Queen's Guards (p. 56). The visitor should glance for a moment at the Queen's bed-chamber and the Hall of Peace, which are found on the right. These are contained in the principal route printed in large type

HALL OF PEACE (114).

After visiting the *Ox-Eye Room*, the visitor should re-enter the Glass Gallery, turn to the left, and reach the Hall of Peace.

On the ceiling France is depicted seated in a car drawn by turtle-doves, preceded by Peace. Over the fireplace is Lemoine's picture : *Young Louis XV giving Peace to France.*

The hall leading to the large apartments of the Queen was re-modelled by Louis XV. It was the game and concert-hall of Marie Leczinska and Marie-Antoinette. The arcade by which it communicates with the Glass Gallery was closed by a great frame, which could be easily removed if the Hall of Peace was required to be joined to the Gallery and Hall of war, for a great ceremony.

From the window opposite the entrance is a splendid view of the Lake of the Swiss Guards (see p. 80).

THE QUEEN'S BED-CHAMBER (115).

The decoration was executed for Queen Marie Leczinska. The visitor will notice the ceiling with its arches, the border of looking-glass (two other mirrors were destroyed in the time of Louis-Philippe), four camayeus painted by Boucher, lintels by Natoire and Detroy, and lastly the portraits of Marie Leczinska by Nattier, and Marie-Antoinette by Mme Vigée-Lebrun.

The Goblin tapestry, by De Troy, is a series from the history of Esther. The *Swooning of Esther*, the *Coronation*, and the *Repast of Assuerus.*

The latter portrait is above the little door by which Marie-Antoinette escaped on the 6th of October, at about 6 o'clock in the morning, when the invasion of the Palace took place. The other door gives access to the *Rooms of the Queen* (described on p. 51).

The bed was placed between these two doors, behind a gilded balustrade, similar to that in the room of Louis XIV. The rings which supported the canopy are still to be seen.

This room was inhabited by Queen Maria-Theresa, wife of Louis XIV, who died in 1683; by the Dauphine of Bavaria, wife of

DOOR OF THE QUEEN'S ROOM

the Grand Dauphin, son of Louis XIV, died in 1690; by the duchess of Burgundy, died in 1712; by Queen Marie Leczinska, died in 1768; by Marie-Antoinette, up till Oct. 6th, 1789. Nineteen princes and princesses of the house of Burgundy were born here.

ROOM OF THE QUEEN'S GUARDS

LARGE ROOM OF THE QUEEN (116).

The Queen, or the Dauphine when there was no queen, held her circle here. The ladies who came to Court were " presented " in this room.

The Goblin tapestry represents the *Anointing of Louis XIV*, the *Alliance with the Swiss*, lastly the *Visit of Louis XIV* accompanied by Colbert, *to the manufactory of the Goblins* To be seen in this composition are several pieces of gold smith's work which decorated the Glass gallery and the large apartments.

ANTE-CHAMBER OF THE GRAND COUVERT (117).

The room, which was formerly the *Ante-Chamber of the Queen*, was used for her repasts " au grand couvert ", to which spectators were freely admitted. The king ate here in public with the Queen severad times. On the ceiling is *the Family of Darius at the feet of Alexander*, a copy of Le Brun's picture in the Louvre.

The tapestry represents the *Surrender of Marsal*, the *Taking of Lille*, and the Audiences to the spanish ambassador and the Pope's Legate for " reperations " made to Louis XIV, in 1662 and 1664.

ROOM OF THE QUEEN'S GUARDS (118).

This beautiful room entirely panelled in marble, has preserved the appearance it presented under Louis XIV. The ceiling, painted by Noël Coypel, represents Jupiter accompanied by Justice and Piety.

The visitor will notice the portrait of the duchess of Burgundy by Santerre, between two busts of princesses of the time of Louis XVI, the busts of Louis XVI and Marie-Antoinette, etc,

HE QUEEN'S STAIRCASE

On the 6ᵗʰ of October 1789, the Palace was invaded by bands armed with pikes who ascended the marble staircase, which reached as far as this room. The body-guard, which had orders not to use arms, fell back into the King's apartment. One of the Queen's Guards was left for dead, across the threshold of the door between this room and the preceding one. Opposite the windows is the marble staircase, called also

THE QUEEN'S STAIRCASE.

The visitor here gains a better idea of the old topography of the Palace. Built in 1682, this beautiful staircase was used in the daily round of the court. At the top, there is on the right the Queen's apartment, and on the left, through a loggia lighted from the marble-court, the King's apartment.

The door of the Hall of the King's Guards is on the side of the bust of Louis XIV. Opposite is the door of the apartment of Mme de Maintenon, secretly married to Louis XIV in 1684, and then almost treated as queen. The staircase leading to the 2ⁿᵈ story was built in the time of Louis-Philippe, and conducts the visitor to the rooms of modern historic painting.

THE CHIMAY ATTIC

These large rooms are four in number. The first is for contemporary documents of the time of the French Revolution.

The visitor will notice among the busts, Mirabeau and Lafayette, by Houdon; the Dauphin (Louis XVII), by Descine; among the portraits, that of Charlotte Corday, painted at the revolutionary tribunal and the Conciergerie by an unskilled but sincere painter, then an officer of the national Guard, and a portrait of Marie-Antoinette in her widow's weeds, as a prisoner in the Temple. To be remarked also is the *Federa-*

tion Fête by Hubert Robert; the famous composition of David : *Marat assassinated*; some dramatic scenes representing the *Day of the 10th of August*, exhibited in the Salon 1895, and the *Sitting of the Convention* where Boissy-d'Anglas saluted the head of the deputy Feraud.

To be seen in the second room is *Bonaparte at the bridge of Arcole*, by Gros; an original cast by Corbet, which is perhaps the finest of the portraits of Napoléon, also the portraits of Mme Récamier and several other noted people, etc.; in the third the series of curious pictures painted by General Lejeune, from his faithful sketches in the Country; in the fourth, the portraits of the Bonaparte family and the two Empresses Josephine and Marie-Louise.

In these small rooms forming a corridor one should stop before the pencilled portraits of the generals of the army in Egypt and the fine collection of sketches by Baron Gérard, under the Consulate and Empire.

Returning to the second room, the visitor should follow the passage with a few steps which will lead him to the south Attic.

THE SOUTH ATTIC

Opposite is a view of the garden of the Tuileries on the day of the marriage of Napoléon to Marie-Louise. The same room includes several pictures of Gros, one of which a sketch filled with portraits (Josephine, the queen Hortense, David, etc). In the second are assembled the dignities of the Empire. In the third group are souvenirs, portraits, painted scenes and drawings which relate to the time of the Restoration. The visitor should remark the addition of interesting series of sketches by Gérard. The Gallery is devoted to the reign of Louis-Philippe. The portraits of Royal family are by Winter-

GALLERY OF BATTLE

halter ; that of the Duke of Orléans was painted by Ingres. Scenes and portraits de Granet, Heim, Isabey, Lami (*Attentat de Fieschi*), etc.

The visitor should return to the Chimay Attic descend to the first story by the same staircase by which he ascended and that leads to the landing of the Queen's staircase.

If he wishes to see the new rooms of the 18th century (p. 55), or if he desires to leave the castle, he should descend the staircase. If he wishes to visit the Gallery of Battles he must turn to the left passing through the great old Guard room (143) and a room of portraits (144), and he will see first the

GREAT GUARD ROOM (143).

This has been entirely modernized. Under the old Monarchy the King used to perform here on Maundy-Thursday the ceremony of the Lord's Supper, washing the feet of twelve poor people. Several court parliaments were held here ; they were the royal seances which called the Parliament of Paris to Versailles to receive King's orders.

There are now three great pictures here : *the Battle of Aboukir* (1799), by Gros, *the Oath of the Army after the distribution of the standards by Napoléon* in 1804, by David, and lastly *the Centenary Fête of the States-General, May 5*[th] 1889 ; M. Roll has here represented the ovation given by the crowd to President Carnot, at Versailles, before the great fountains of Neptune, and has painted many well-known faces.

The dying Napoleon, by Vela, was bought at the Exhibition of 1867. The bronzes of the furniture are among the finest existing specimens of the style of the First Empire.

ROOM (144).

The visitor passes through a little room, where the pictures recall the episodes of the Revolutionary Wars. There are two important canvasses of Eugène Lamy, *Hondschoote* and *Wattignies,* September and October 1793.

ROOM OF 1792 (146).

This is the old hall of the Swiss-Hundred, now sacred to the memory of the campaign of Valmy and Jemmapes, which saved France from invasion. The portraits are those of military personages who took part in this campaign, and who afterwards become generals or marshals of the Empire, or sovereigns, as Bernadotte and Louis-Philippe. They are for the most part renovations of portraits subsequent to the time.

At the side are small rooms containing watercolours, which illustrate the campaigns of the Republic and the Empire.

PRINCES' STAIRCASE (147).

This staircase was used in connexion with the South Wing, occupied by the princes of the blood. On the landing is the entrance to the

GALLERY OF BATTLES (148).

This immense gallery built in 1836, under Louis-Philippe; is 390 feet long (150 feet longer than the Glass-Gallery) and 42 feet broad. It stands on the side of the apartments of the royal family, and countains a set, commencing at the left, of majestic compositions on the principal battles in French history. The finest work is *Saint Louis at the Battle of Taillebourg,*

THE DAUPHIN'S LIBRARY

by Delacroix. The three last pictures, *Iena*, *Friedland*, and *Wagram*, are by Horace Vernet. Near the entrance is the popular picture by Georges Bertrand, *Patrie*, a symbolic episode of the war of 1870. The Gallery is decorated with 16 bronze tablets on which are inscribed the names of princes, admirals, constables, marshals and generals who died fighting for their country, and also with 82 busts reproducing the features of some of these heroes.

At the end of the Gallery is a room called the *Hall of* 1830 (149), where several paintings recall the Revolution of 1830, which made Louis-Philippe (Duke of Orleans, and future founder of the Museum of Versailles), King of the French.

The visitor must now retrace his steps as far as *the Princes' Staircase*.

If he wishes to see first the ground-floor of the main body of the Palace, the new rooms of portraits and marshals, he must return as far as the Queen's Staircase, descend and turn to the left (p. 66).

If he intends visiting the Galleries of the Empire, he descends the Princes' Staircase, and, passing the sculpture-gallery known as the Gallery of Tombs (81), turns twice to the left and enters the picture-galleries on the side of the park.

GALLERIES OF THE EMPIRE (68-80).

In reality, the first of these thirteen halls illustrates campaigns of the Republic.

The pictures commence with the year 1796, and represent the principal episodes of the campaigns of Italy, Egypt, Marengo, Austerlitz, Iena, Friedland, Spain and Wagram, and many historic deeds and ceremonies of the time. Most of the pictures, of great historic interest, were painted by the order of Napoleon I.

There are everywhere explanatory labels, and chronological order is regularly followed, except in the pictures of general Lejeune, the installation of which is recent, and in the Marengo Hall, situated quite at the end of the wing.

This part of the Museum serves as offices and promenades for the Deputies and Senators, when the Congress meets to elect a President of the Republic.

The visitor can either return by the same way or by the sculpture-gallery, and then reaches the

VESTIBULE OF THE PRINCES' COURT.

This vestibule gives access to the park, on the terrace of the Orangery. The open door opposite the exit is an entrance to the ground-floor of the main body of the Palace.

The visitor crosses several passages filled with sculpture (40, 39,38), passes the foot of the Queen's staircase and enters on the left the

NEW GALLERIES OF THE XVIII. CENTURY (§ 51).

It is absolutely necessary to visit these costly galleries, *otherwise one can have no idea of the riches of art contained in the Museum.* This important collection of later years is devoted to documents, portraits, pictures, etc., which relate to the history of France during the xviii century. It is to be continued (the ancient period finding its place in the Northern Attic and the Maintenon apartment, and the modern period in the Chimay and Southern Attics. All the decoration of the apartments was destroyed in the time of Louis Philip for fitting up the Ancient Museum. Two beautiful fire places have been placed in rooms n°° 43 and 45. One of them is in carved bronze and both figured in the apartments of Marie Antoinette. Nearly all the pictures are worthy of attention. The most remarkable in the first rooms being the portrait of Louis XV as a child by Rigaud, the Regent by Santerre, the view of the Sainte-Chapelle and the Court of the Palace at Paris such as it was in 17 15. with an infinity of small personages, the *Anointing of Louis XV at Reims* done during the time, the canvases of Belle representing the little Infant the first affianced of Louis XV, and Marie Leczinska and the Dauphin by Nattier, and some admirable portraits by Rigaud, Largillière, Socqué, Van Loo, Roslin, Drouais and Duplessis.

One portion of these rooms less destroyed than the others, the first of which is a Library, formed the beautiful apartment of the Dauphin.

APARTMENT OF THE DAUPHIN (47-50).

These rooms were in the time of Louis XIV the apartment of Monseigneur (called the Grand Dauphin). They were occupied by the Regent, Philip of Orleans, who died in gallery n° 49, after by the Dauphin, son of Louis XV, and it is from the fitting out of the suite for this prince in 1747 that date nearly all the beautiful decorative fragments still to be seen. In the Grand Cabinet, a magnificent room in the angle of six windows with a frieze panelling by Oudry, is gathered together the most precious collection in the world of pictures by Nattier, all portraits of the ladies of France daughters of Louis XV. Here also are to be seen the original marbles of both Lemoyne and Houdon.

In the gilt room (the Dauphin's bedroom) is preserved a carved mirror and fireplace by Caffieri representing Flora and Zephyr; the portrait of the Dauphine is by Natoire, that of

APARTEMENTS OF THE DAUPHIN

Louis XV in Goblin tapestry is after L. M. Van Loo. The three pictures of Nattier should be remarked.

LOWER GALLERY (51).

This hall situated below the " Galerie des Glaces" was used as a direct passage from the Marble Court to the gardens : here is to be found the admirable Louis XVI by Houdon as well as two celebrated pieces of furniture : the bureau of Louis XVI and the jewel chest of Marie Antoinette.

MESDAMES' APARTMENT (52-54).

These were formerly the bathrooms in the time of Louis XV. The daughters of Louis XV occupied them later in the reign of Louis XVI and all the pictures relate to that time.

There have been added recently several celebrated portraits of Marie Antoinette (of which the large portrait with the children was painted by Mme Vigée-le-Brun in 1787), those of Madame Adelaïde and Madame Victoire by Mme Mabille-Quiard, that of Louis XV par Callet, the *Gardens of Versailles* by Hubert-Robert, etc.

One passes from the Lower Gallery into a vestibule with columns placed in the centre of the Château, under the room of Louis XIV and from there to the right and left one enters the gallery of the new acquisitions; continuing to the left one reaches the Chapel.

GALLERY OF THE NEW ACQUISITIONS (22 and 33).

The works of art recently bought or accepted as gifts by the Museum are here exhibited before being placed in the historic series to which they belong. This exhibition which changes from time to time is always interesting.

GALLERY OF ROYAL RESIDENCES (34).

This gallery contains an interesting collection of ancient views of royal castles. In it one sees the shrubberies of Versailles, many of which no longer exist, also views of the Castle as it was in the time of Louis XIV and in the beginning of the reign of Louis XV. On the right one will notice the view of Versailles taken from the level of the water before the construction of the Galerie des Glaces, and on the left close to the entrance a curious general view of the side of the courtyards.

There is a passage leading to the Queen's staircase at the foot of which one can *leave the castle.*

BUILDINGS OF THE SENATE (OPERA) AND HOUSE OF DEPUTIES.

Beyond the Museum there are still two halls to be visited in the Palace. The first is reached by the rue des Réservoirs, by the door over which is written the word *Senat*; it is the old court Opera built by Gabriel in the reign of Louis XV and inaugurated for the marriage fêtes of Marie-Antoinette and the Dauphin in 1770. It was here that the celebrated banquet of the body guards took place on October 1st 1789, which excited great indignation in Paris and was the cause of the terrible " days of October ".

The hall is still very fine; the sculptures are by Pajou. Unfortunately Louis-Philippe changed the tone of all the paintings, and later on the installation of the National Assembly in 1871 on their return from Bordeaux entirely altered the character of the hall.

According to the Constitution of 1875 which instituted two Houses of Parliament, this building was destined for the sittings of the Senate which has not met here since 1878, the date of the return of the Houses to Paris.

The entrance of the *House of Deputies* is on the other side of the Palace from the Princes' Court.

The care-takers can be distinguished by their red waistcoats. It was built in 1875 in the centre of a large court-yard and can seat 825 persons. It is used for the meetings of the National Assembly or Congress (Members of the House of Deputies and Senators united) and has witnessed the election of the last French Presidents.

SALLE DU JEU DE PAUME (TENNIS-COURT).

This building is open to the public like the Museum, of which it is a dependence. It is reached by the rue Gambetta, the rue du Vieux-Versailles and the rue du Jeu-de-Paume.

The hall of the " Jeu-de-Paume ", where the Revolution of June 20ᵗʰ 1789 began be the celebrated oath of the Deputies of the Tiers-Etat, was entirely restored in 1880. The statue of Bailly, reading the terms of the Oath, is to by remarked, also twenty busts of the most eminent members of the Constituant Assembly and a picture not historically accurate representing the scene of the Oath according to the sketch which is in the Louvre. Glass cabinets containing prints, autographs and souvenirs form a little Museum especially devoted to the history of the Revolution concerning Versailles.

THE TOWN-LIBRARY.

Going to the Jeu-de-Paume by the rue Gambetta one passes first a large building dating from Louis XIV, now the Military Hospital and which was formerly the *Servants' Hall*, that is to say the whole of the Dependents of the Castle and the Royal kitchen, then before the school of the Artillery and the Engineers, former residence of the Minister for War, at last before the Town-Library.

This Library, one of the finest in France, occupies the former residence of the Minister of Foreign Affairs.

The gallery of the ground-floor, all the frieze panels of which were painted by Van Blarenberghe, is just the same now as it was at the time of the Ministry of the Duc du Choiseul. The Treaty of Versailles was signed in the Gallery in which one finds the portrait of this-Minister.

The collections contain a portion of the private libraries of Louis XIV, Louis XV and Louis XVI, the daughters of Louis XV, Marie-Antoinette at Trianon, Madam Elizabeth at Montreuil; the books of Madam du Barry and the Royal Residence of Saint-Cyr, etc. A portion of the rich bindings is on view.

On the second storey is a small Municipal Museum showing more particularly an interesting collection of mouldings the work of Jean Houdon, born at Versailles.

SIGHTS OF THE TOWN

Electric trams enable one to make a rapid tour of the Town.

The one starting from the bottom of the rue Gambetta at the Orangery gate serves the two stations. It passes first the Cathedral Church of Saint-Louis, where the order of the Clergy solemnly declared its union with the Third State which took place there, June 22ᵈ 1789, after the Oath of the Game of Tennis. Statue of the Abbé de l'Epée, born at Versailles. The tram also passes the new Hotel de Ville and the residence of the Prefect which was the Residence of Thiers and Mac-Mahon as Presidents of the Republic. The same line leads to Duplessis Square where there is a monument to Houdon by Messrs Tony Noël and Favier.

There is also to be seen the place Hoche ornamented by a rather poor monument of the General peace-mediator of Vendée, born at Versailles; and the Church of Notre-Dame, for a long time the only parish Church of the Town. It was built under Louis XIV by Mansart, whose monument is in the first Chapel on the left, and also the one to Quintinie, gardener to Louis XIV. In the same Chapel is a monument raised to the memory of the Comte de Vergennes, Minister of Louis XVI, and another containing the heart of Hoche. The sculptured pulpit in the Church dates from Louis XIV.

Close to the Church of Saint-Louis, in the rue du Potager is the former royal kitchen-garden founded by la Quintinie and now the National School of Horticulture. The entrance is public.

Amongst the former hotels one remarks in many streets, one deserving of special mention is that of Madam de Pompadour, rue des Reservoirs, now become the middle part of the well known Hôtel des Reservoirs.

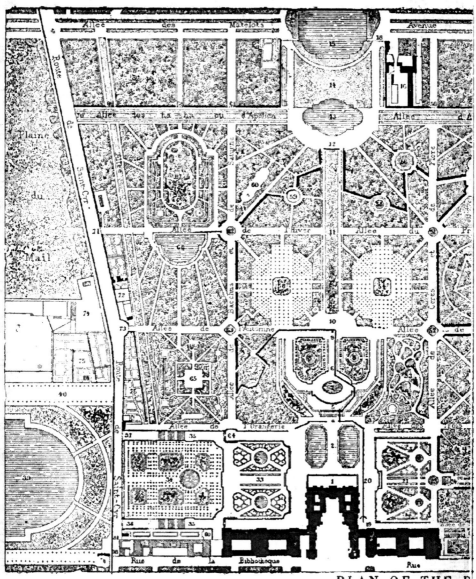

PLAN OF THE P

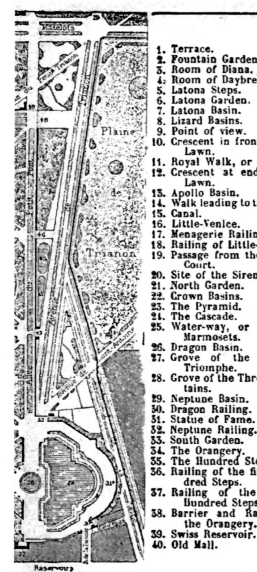

1. Terrace.
2. Fountain Gardens.
3. Room of Diana.
4. Room of Daybreak.
5. Latona Steps.
6. Latona Garden.
7. Latona Basin.
8. Lizard Basins.
9. Point of view.
10. Crescent in front of the Lawn.
11. Royal Walk, or Lawn.
12. Crescent at end of the Lawn.
13. Apollo Basin.
14. Walk leading to the Canal.
15. Canal.
16. Little-Venice.
17. Menagerie Railing.
18. Railing of Little-Venice.
19. Passage from the Chapel-Court.
20. Site of the Siren-Basin.
21. North Garden.
22. Crown Basins.
23. The Pyramid.
24. The Cascade.
25. Water-way, or walk of Marmosets.
26. Dragon Basin.
27. Grove of the Arc-de-Triomphe.
28. Grove of the Three Fountains.
29. Neptune Basin.
30. Dragon Railing.
31. Statue of Fame.
32. Neptune Railing.
33. South Garden.
34. The Orangery.
35. The Hundred Steps.
36. Railing of the first Hundred Steps.
37. Railing of the second Hundred Steps.
38. Barrier and Railing of the Orangery.
39. Swiss Reservoir.
40. Old Mall.
41. Water Theatre.
42. Children's Basin.
43. Railing of Ceres.
44. The Star.
45. Reservoirs of Jambettes.
46. Railing of Jambettes.
47. Sheaf Basin, Obelisk or corn-stalk basin.
48. Railing of Apollo.
49. Railing of the Little Bridge.
50. Railing of Flora.
51. Basin of Flora.
52. Basin of Ceres.
53. Baths of Apollo.
54. North Quincunx.
55. The Domes.
56. The Encelade.
57. The Pebbles or Ball-Room.
58. South Quincunx.
59. The Colonnade.
60. Chestnut Hall.
61. Railing of Saturn.
62. Basin of Saturn.
63. Basin of Bacchus.
64. Royal Gate of the Orangery.
65. Grove of the Queen.
66. The Mirror.
67. King's Garden.
68. Wall-opening in the King's Garden.
69. Railing of the Maids of Honour.
70. Railing of the Pheasantry.
71. Railing of the play-ground.
72. Play-ground.
73. Railing of the mall.
74. The Stand.
75. The Conservatory.
76. Reservoirs.
77. Roulette Pavilion.
78. Post of the Park-watchmen.
79. Railing of the Trianon.
80. Little Orangery.
81. Railing of the Little Orangery.

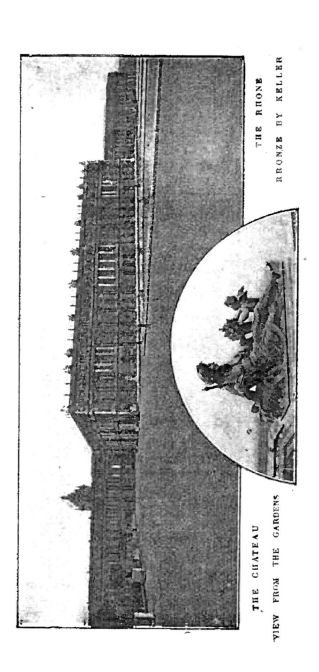

THE CHATEAU
VIEW FROM THE GARDENS

THE RHONE
BRONZE BY KELLER

III

THE PARK

GENERAL VIEW OF THE GARDENS.

On entering the Park, the visitor walks in front of the Palace and arrives at the Fountain Garden.

Standing in the centre, at the edge of the staircase, he has before him the general view of the Gardens. At the foot of the stairs, the Latona Basin, then the grand garden of Latona, at the end of which opens a long perspective formed by the Lawn, the Apollo Basin, and the Grand Canal.

On either side of the Fountain Garden are : — to the left, the South Garden, the Orangery, and, outside the railings, the Swiss basin; to the right, the North Garden, the water-

way or Marmoset-walk, the Dragon Basin, and Basin of Nep
tune.   Fourteen groves, six on the left, eight on the right,
complete the Gardens of Versailles.

TERRACE VASE

The word *Park*, in general use, is inexact.   In Louis XIV's time
a much more extensive piece of land, enclosed by walls, and
comprising more than 4344 acres was called *Park* or *Little Park*.
The large Park which was used for the Royal Hunt comprised
16 344 acres and was 27 miles in circuit.

The *Gardens* of Versailles were designed under Louis XIII
by Jacques Boyceau, to complete the work of the architect
Lemercier.   Under Louis XIV, the celebrated Lenôtre enlarged

and perfected this design, and the Italian engineer Francine constructed the celebrated fountains, still in use.

The appearance of the gardens is very much as it was in

GROUP OF CHILDREN IN THE FOUNTAIN-GARDENS

Lenôtre's time, save for some alterations made in the eighteenth century.

FAÇADE OF THE PALACE FROM THE GARDENS.

From the Fountain-Gardens, the visitor obtains the most

majestic view of the Palace, with its projecting centre piece and its two great wings.

The length of the façade is 1350 feet; the extreme length, comprising the façades on the side of the principal building, is 2145 feet. From no one point can a complete view be obtained.

· There is throughout ground-floor, first floor and attic. The 96 ornamental statues are 7 feet 7 inches in height. The vases and trophies decorating the balustrade had fallen into ruins and were restored under the first Empire. It is proposed to replace them by others which shall more suitably break the monotony of a long line.

THE FOUNTAIN GARDEN AND ITS TWO CABINETS.

· The ornamentation of the Fountain Garden presents the finest collection of bronzes in the world. The two basins are lined with a white marble rim bearing sixteen magnificent statues of French rivers and streams, of nymphs, and groups of children.

These bronzes, modelled by the greatest sculptors of the time of Louis XIV, were cast at Paris by the brothers Keller. Two of the finest figures are those which face the Hall of War, *the Garonne* and *the Dordogne* by Coysevox.

The two lateral fountains are adorned with bronzes by the same founders representing realistic animal battles.

That on the right (turning one's back to the Palace), is the *Room of Diana*, so called from the statue of the huntress .Diana, by Desjardins, which stands at the side. The animals are by Houzeau. One of the most beautiful statues in the Park is on the left of the fountain: it is *Air*, by Lehongre, a female figure resting on clouds and wrapped in drapery, which she holds aloft over her head.

At the left is the *Cabinet of Day-break*, with animals by

THE ORANGERY

Van Clève. The neighbouring statue, wnich gives it its name, has a star on its head and a cock at its feet. It is the work of G. Marsy.

The two large marble vases placed at the corners of the terrace, at the base of the Palace, are works of art no less remarkable; that on the left (looking towards the Palace) is by Coysevox (bas-reliefs on the pre-eminence of France recognized by Spain, and the defeat of the Turks in Hungary); that on the right is by Tuby (Louis XIV triumphant by the peace of Aix-la-Chapelle, and that of Nimegen, 1679).

SOUTH GARDEN AND TERRACE OF THE ORANGERY.

This garden is bordered with marble slabs supporting bronze vases. The visitor will notice on the central steps two exquisite groups, each representing a marble Sphinx with a little bronze Cupid. On the steps to the right is a recumbent figure of *Ariadne*, after the ancient Statue in the Vatican Museum.

The box-edgings form complicated designs which give a good idea of the plan of old French gardens.

The Terrace is situated over the great galleries of the Orangery (erected by Mansart in 1686), which served as a prison for the Communists in 1871.

The Swiss basin was excavated between 1679 and 1683 by the regiment of Swiss Guards. It is about 2258 feet long, and 760 broad. The woods in the background are on the slopes of Satory.

After having inspected the Orangery from above, and the great stairs called the Cent-Marches (Hundred steps), the visitor returns to the large steps in front of the Palace and descends to the Latona Garden.

LATONA BASIN

6

GARDEN AND BASIN OF LATONA.

The great garden of Latona comprises the two Lizard basins and that of Latona. The leaden sculpture of these basins has been regilt; nearly all the figures of the park fountains were thus finished in Louis XIV's time.

The marble group in the basin of Latona represents the goddess with her two children, Apollo and Diana. She is imploring Jupiter to punish the Lycians, who insulted her when she asked them for a drink, and he changes them into frogs, lizards and tortoises. This metamorphosis is represented in groups of gilded lead.

On each side of the gardens is a slope ornamented with shaped yews and statues. At the foot of these are two beautiful recumbent figures : on the right, the Shell Nymph, by Coysevox (a copy); on the left, the Dying Gladiator, a copy from the antique in the Capitol museum, Rome.

In the crescent in front of the Lawn (10) before the garden of Latona, are four groups after the antique : on the right Castor and Pollux, Arria and Pœtus; on the left, Papirius and his mother Laocoon and his sons.

In the centre of the crescent is found what is called the *Point of View* (9). It was to this poin. Louis XIV used to conduct the great personages who visited Versailles in order to give them the best view of the gardens.

The visitor has now before him the

LAWN, OR ROYAL WALK (14).

This beautiful walk, the most frequented in the Park, is 1079 feet long, and 208 feet broad. It is decorated with twelve statues and the same number of white marble vases.

THE BELL NYMPH

furning his back on the Palace and walking towards the Apollo basin, the visitor has on his left : Fidelity, the Venus of Richelieu (by Legros, after an antique at the Chateau of Richelieu), Fawn and Kid, Dido on her funeral-pyre, Amazon after the antique, Achilles at Scyros.

The statues on the right are : Deceit, Juno (an antique statue). Hercules and Telephus, the Venus of Medici, Cyparis, Artemisa.

Those who only wish to see the principal curiosities of the Park traverse the Lawn as far as the Colonnade.

The groves on the left are : *the Rockeries, the Queen's Glade,* and *the King's Garden.* The first is reached by the little walk behind the statue of the Dying Gladiator.

THE ROCKERIES OR BALL-ROOM (57).

This glade was used as a ball-room in the garden fêtes given by Louis XIV. The cascades produce a curious effect when the great fountains are playing.

On the other side of the large walk by which the visitor leaves the Rockeries is

THE QUEEN'S GLADE (65).

It was designed in Louis XVI's time in place of the old maze of Louis XIV.

In the large walk at the end of the glade, which starts at one of the doors of the Orangery, is found the Basin of Bacchus (63), and further on the Basin of Saturn (62).

On the left is

THE KING'S GARDEN (47).

The large fountain in front of this garden enclosed by railings is called the Mirror. The garden itself, laid out in English fashion, was not made and planted till 1817, under Louis XVIII. It is remarkable for its trees and wealth of flowers. There is only one entrance, and on leaving the visitor returns to the Basin of Saturn, whence he can regain the Lawn or the Colonnade.

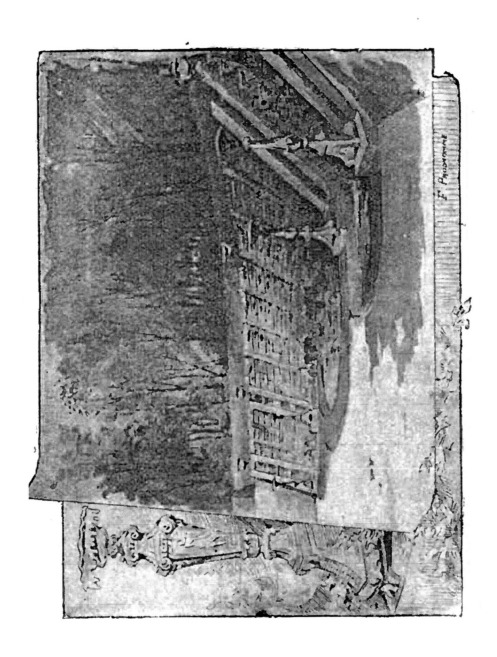

THE COLONNADE (59).

Following the Royal Walk, the fifth path on the left leads to the Colonnade. In the centre of this Colonnade, designed by Mansart, is a group representing the *Capture of Proserpine by Pluto, King of the Nether World;* the same scene is depicted in bas-relief on the pedestal. This masterpiece is the work of Girardon.

GROVE OF DOMES (55).

Nearly opposite the path leading to the Colonnade is one to the Grove of Domes. - This has been recently restored. It is decorated with fine statues and trophies of arms sculptured in bas-relief by Girardon, Guérin and Mazeline. The name is derived from two pavilions surmounted with gilded domes that were formerly here.

BASIN OF APOLLO (13).

The group in lead in this basin was made by Tuby, after designs by Lebrun, so as to stand out amid the sparkling spray of the fountains.

It represents the Car of Apollo, the Sun-God, who, as Greek mythology relates, rose from Ocean every morning to illumine the earth, and every evening plunged in its waves. It is well known that Louis XIV had the Sun for his emblem, and that poets and courtiers compared their master to Apollo.

Now-a-days the Car of Apollo is popularly styled " the Car stuck in the mud ".

At the right of the Canal-head is a boat-house, where boats are let out on hire (18). The large walk (Sailors' Avenue) opposite the landing-stage, brings us in five minutes to the Trianon railing (79).

The Trianon is also reached from the Basin of Apollo, by the Apollo Walk, and railing of the Petit-Pont (49).

THE COLONNADE

ENCELADE GROVE (56).

Returning towards the Palace, the second path on the left of the Royal Walk leads to the Encelade Basin.

Titan in revolt against Jupiter is represented just as the thunderbolt strikes him, his giant limbs crushed beneath masses of rock. A grand jet of water is emitted from the colossal figure's mouth. The sculpture, in lead, is the work of B. Marsy.

THE OBÉLISK OR HUNDRED-STALKS (47).

The grove of this name is reached by the same walk as the Encelade, after crossing the large path known as the Flora Walk. In the centre of a large basin is a clump of reeds whence issue jets of water forming a pyramid or obelisk. It is also called the " Sheaf ".

The visitor regains the Flora Walk and Basin (51), where is one entrance to the Star-Grove, sometimes called the Maze, which is of little interest. Retracing his steps along the walk opposite the figure of Flora as far as the Ceres Basin (52), he enters, on the right, the Grove of Apollo.

On the left is situated the Basin of Children (42), decorated with a charming group in lead of little swimmers.

GROVE OF THE BATHS OF APOLLO (53).

This English grove, the only one in the Park of Versailles, was only begin in Louis XVI's time, 1778, after designs by Hubert Robert, when the new taste which then inspired the Trianon began to realise that the severe style of Lenôtre's gardens was old-fashioned.

An artificial rock forms the entrance to the Palace of Tethys,

CAR OF APOLLO, AND GREAT CANAL

goddess of the sea, where Apollo is supposed to come every evening to rest after illumining the earth.

A fine group in white marble represents six nymphs of Tethys in attendance on the god, presenting him perfumes. His horses are at rest at the foot of the rock. Save for three figures by Regnaudin, the group is the work of Girardon; it was made about 1672, to represent the Sun-King by a flattering allegory.

THE NORTH GARDEN (21).

The exit is on the left at the top of the grove, by a crossway where there are some beautiful marble hot-baths; the visitor then takes the turning on the right at the edge of the North Garden.

In the centre of this walk is the *Pyramid Fountain* (23)

THE BATHS OF APOLLO

(commonly known as "the Boiling Pot"), the leaden sculpture of which, crabs, dolphins and tritons, is by Girardon.

If the visitor cares to ascend the stairs to the Terrace in front of the Palace, he will notice two bronze statues, after the antique, both seated figures, one representing Venus (bearing the signature of Coysevox), and the other "the Grinder", from the Museum of Florence.

CASCADE OF THE WATER-WAY (24).

The visitor follows the path below the Pyramid called the Water-way. The fine central bas-relief in bronzed lead, in the square basin where the water falls in a cascade, is by Girardon, and represents the Nymphs of the Bath.

WATER-WAY OR WALK OF MARMOSETS (25).

The walk is ornamented with fourteen little fountains of white marble, each a group of three children in bronze supporting a vase of Languedoc marble. These groups are popularly known as the "Marmosets". There are only seven in the walk, these being imperceptibly repeated on either side.

THE DRAGON BASIN (26).

Around the Dragon Basin eight other groups of children in bronze form companions to the "Marmosets". The leaden sculpture in this basin is quite modern, and unfortunately very different from the other work in the Park. It was modelled after prints.

On the right is the entrance to the *Grove of the Triumphal Arch* (27), of modern arrangement; there is nothing worth seeing but a group in lead representing "France triumphant between Spain and the Empire", by Tuby and Coysevox.

FOUNTAIN OF NEPTUNE (29).

The fountains of this magnificent basin and the ornamental lead-work were restored in 1889.

FRANCE TRIUMPHANT

FOUNTAIN OF NEPTUNE

The three groups on the level of the water represent, the central, Neptune, God of the Sea, and his wife Amphitrite, that on the right, Ocean, that on the left, Proteus, another sea-god. These works were finished under Louis XV, by Adam, Lemoine and Bouchardon.

A great crowd gathers here on the days when the great fountains play to watch the grand effects. It is the most interesting point of the large fountains, and that where the final display takes place. Every year some evening fêtes are given here.

The buildings seen above the Basin of Neptune and the other side of the rue des Reservoirs are *the Hôtel des Réservoirs*, former residence of Mme de Pompadour, and the municipal Theatre, built under Louis XVI.

The visitor re-enters the town by the Dragon Gate, and is not far from the Railway (right bank). The opposite route leads to the Trianon in ten minutes.

VASE OF THE NEPTUNE BASIN

IV

THE TRIANONS

A visit to the two Trianons is necessary to any foreigner who wishes to have a true idea of the beauties of Versailles. In which case he will do well to reserve it for a second day, because he will not have too much time in giving the whole of the first to the Chateau, Museum and Park; as as much as that is necessary to travel over them in order to see them in detail.

Although "Les Trianons" can only be considered as belonging to Versailles, they are sufficiently interesting of themselves to be worth visiting more leisurely than is sometimes possible. As one is obliged to traverse the interiors very rapidly on account of the great number of visitors and the small number of guides, there are the two parks which we recommend to be seen at leisure.

That of " Grand Trianon " is not so celebrated as " Little Trianon ". It affords nevertheless some most interesting points, a large parterre à la française, quiet and magnificent alleys and in the south part a terrace from which is an admirable view of the Grand Canal of Versailles, one of the arms of which ends there.

The national estate of Trianon is a quarter of an hour's distance from Versailles, or a few minutes drive. Those who only desire to see one of the two Trianons should decide on the Smaller which is more interesting on account of the souvenirs of Marie-Antoinette (see page 114). In this case it is necessary to inform the coachman, or, if on foot, after passing the railing of the estate turn to the right immediately behind the porter's lodge, and then take the broad walk on the left.

THE GREAT TRIANON

HISTORY.

The adjective which qualifies *Grand* Trianon was not employed until the time when Louis XV at the end of his reign founded the *Little* Trianon. Up till then the simple name of Trianon which often appears in the memoirs and historical works was applied to the estate and the palaces built by Louis XIV close to Versailles and destined like " Marly le Roi " as places of rest for the King in his continual public life.

Shortly after the first works that he ordered to be done at

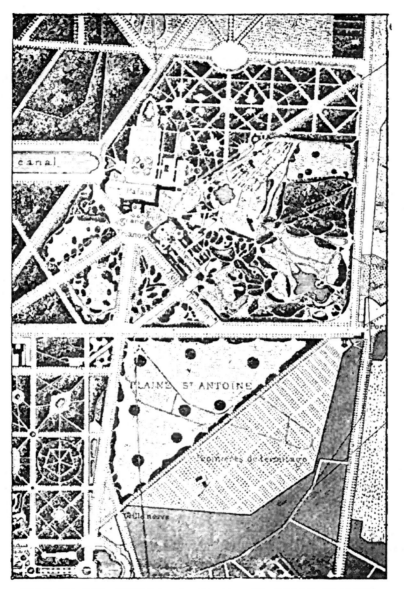

canal

Palais
Grand
Trianon

Trianon

PLAINE St ANTOINE

Pépinières de l'ermitage

Ville neuve

PLAN OF THE GROUNDS OF THE GRAND TRIANON

Versailles were finished, in order to increase his Park Louis XIV bought the hamlet bearing the name of Trianon and with it all the land with which it was surrounded. He did not long delay in building a little pleasure house which was built in 1670 and surrounded by beautiful gardens full of rare flowers. As the house was so remarkable for its decoration in plaques, vases and ornaments in China, it was called the *Porcelain Trianon*. It lasted seventeen years and was the admiration of the age.

The Court and the Government having been installed at Versailles in the year 1682, it was natural that Trianon should participate in the enlargements then done. Mansard demolished the Porcelain Trianon and built between 1687 and 1691 a real palace of one storey with a flat Italian roof which is the same we see to-day. The amount of marble was prodigious and there were numberless workmen employed in Versailles at both the interior and exterior decoration. During all the latter part of his reign Louis XIV made numerous stays there in the Apartment of the left wing of the palace. Madam de Maintenon and the amiable Duchess of Bourgogne were both fond of Trianon. The Czar Peter the Great stayed there during his journey in France from June 3rd to June 6th 1717. Louis XV gave Trianon to Queen Marie Leczinska. He stayed there himself pretty frequently during the second half of his reign and established amongst other things a botanical garden which was useful to science and became celebrated for the experiments of Bernard de Jussieu.

In 1794 Trianon escaped the sale with which it was threatened as National property and the furniture only was sold.

Napoleon I who thought of restoring the property, had Trianon refurnished and often stayed there, principally after his divorce from Josephine (from December 16th to December 26th 1809). Louis Philippe made great changes in the arrangement of the

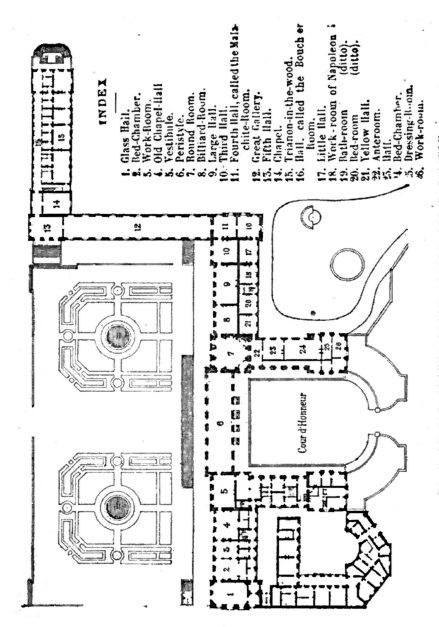

INDEX

1. Glass Hall.
2. Bed-Chamber.
3. Work-Room.
4. Old Chapel-Hall.
5. Vestibule.
6. Peristyle.
7. Round Room.
8. Billiard-Room.
9. Large Hall.
10. Third Hall.
11. Fourth Hall, called the Malachite-Room.
12. Great Gallery.
13. Fifth Hall.
14. Chapel.
15. Trianon-in-the-wood.
16. Hall, called the Boucher Room.
17. Little Hall.
18. Work-room of Napoleon i
19. Bath-room   (dito).
20. Bed-room   (dito).
21. Yellow Hall.
22. Anteroom.
23. Hall.
24. Bed-Chamber.
25. Dressing-Room.
26. Work-room.

Cour d'Honneur

PLAN OF THE GROUND FLOOR OF THE GREAT TRIANON

apartments, and resided there several summers, after 1836, with his family and the Court.

The historic furniture and the greater number of the works of art in both the Trianons are controlled by the administration of the National Furniture. The pictures and sculpture form a little museum annexed to the Museum of Versailles.

LARGE APARTMENTS.

The visitor can only enter the Villa of the Trianon when accompanied by a keeper of the National Palaces (a different administration to that of Versailles), who gives the necessary explanations. The following will complete these from an artistic point of view.

GLASS HALL (1).

This room, for the decoration of which Louis XIV spent 10 500 livres in purchasing Venetian mirrors, possesses a splendid fireplace of red marble relieved with bronze, in Louis XVI style.

BED-CHAMBER (2) AND WORK-ROOM (3).

The first of these two rooms was formerly the room of Louis XIV. Among the mythological pictures of the second, notice one by Natoire, " Allegory on the birth of a princess (time of Louis XV) whom Hymen brings to France ". The furniture of all the rooms dates from about the time of Louis-Philippe.

OLD CHAPEL-HALL (4).

The altar was placed in the recess opposite the central window. In the time of Louis-Philippe, the Chapel was moved to that part of the Villa called Trianon-in-the-wood. Two portraits by J.-B. Vanloo represent Louis XV and Marie Leczinska in their youth.

THE GREAT TRIANON (LEFT WING)

VESTIBULE (5).

In Louis XIV's time this room gave access to the King's apartments. Over the fireplace is a picture oɪ the Mignard school representing a trophy of arms oɪ the " Grand Roi ", with his motto, *Nec pluribus impar.*

PERISTYLE (6).

The peristyle, decorated with pilasters and marble columns was formerly open and gave direct access to the gardens. Napoleon I had it closed by glass windows. It was here.that Marshal Bazaine was tried by Court Martial.

Among the statues notice the *Boy extracting a thorn* and the *Cockel Player*, marbles after the antique, an equestrian statue oɪ Louis XIV, in bronze, and the group in Vela marble, *France and Italy*, presented to the Empress Eugenie by the ladies of Milan, after the war of 1859.

LARGE ROUND ROOM (7).

This finely decorated room served as the Chapel under Louis XVI. The armchairs and stools are in Beauvais tapestry (a series of La Fontaine's fables). It is decorated with pictures by Monnoyer, Desportes and Blain of Fontenay (vases oɪ flowers and American fruits), and with a *Fawn*, a bronze after the antique.

BILLIARD-ROOM (8).

This was the music room in Louis XIV's time. Napoleon I had it converted into a billiard-room.

In the wainscotting notice a bust-portrait of Louis XV by Vanloo, and Marie Leczinska, by Nattier.

LARGE HALL OF LOUIS-PHILIPPE (9).

This has been decorated with mythological pictures by Seb. Leclerc, Bon Boulogne, Antoine and Noël Coypel, Verdier, La-rosse, etc.

GRAND TRIANON

Over the fireplace is a bas-relief, an old cameo in oriental alabaster, the subject being sacrifice to the god Pan.

Notice the beautiful vases of Japanese porcelain.

HALL (10).

There are four beautiful pieces of flower painting by Monnoyer, a picture by Lafosse, *Apollo and Thetis*, and some fine old furniture : consoles of carved wood, a Louis XIV table (unfortunately regilded), a cabinet of carved and gilded wood, touched up with white, Louis XIV style, etc.

MALACHITE HALL (11).

The name comes from the malachite objects presented by Czar Alexander I to the emperor Napoleon I, after the peace of Tilsit ; these are — the cup in the centre of the hall, the two chandeliers, the two cupboards and the console. The other articles were acquired by King Charles X.

The armchairs and stools are of Beauvais tapestry.

The portrait of Henry IV by Hersent is a modern work. The four other full-length portraits are interesting. They are : Louis XIV, one of the Rigaud school, Louis XV, by Vanloo, Louis of France, Dauphin, by Natoire, and Louis XVI, by Duplessis.

GREAT GALLERY (12).

This gallery communicates with the central portion of the Villa and the wing called Trianon-in-the-wood. Under Louis-Philippe it became the great dining-hall, decorated with pictures of divers kinds, mostly mediocres, statuettes, vases of Sèvres porcelain, etc. There are also reduced models of Trajan's Column and one of the temples of Pœstum. The pink-marble bowls were used to cool wine in iced water.

The following hall and the Chapel, built under Louis-Philippe, are of little interest, as is the Trianon-in-the-wood (15) where the princes of the blood in the time of Louis XIV,

DINING ROOM

and Louis XV lived during the King's stay. These apartments entirely dismantled of their furniture, are not open to the public.

HALL OF SPRINGS, CALLED THE BOUCHER-ROOM (16).

This room, which in Louis XIV's time overlooked a little wood traversed by streams, called the Garden of Springs, was converted into a library by Napoleon I.

It is ornamented with four great pictures by Boucher, representing : *Neptune and Amymone, Venus and Vulcan, the Fortune-teller* and *Fishing*. Notice too the *View of the ancient aqueducts of the Palace of Nero, Rome*, by Hubert Robert, and a clock of gilded bronze in the form of a basket of flowers, with a circular enamelled dial, in which the hours are shown in the centre of the corolla of a flower.

SMALL APARTMENTS (17-21).

These apartments were inhabited by M⁻ de Maintenon, by Louis XV, by Stanislas Leczinski, King of Poland, by M⁻ de Pompadour, and finally by Napoleon I, who gave them their present appearance and furniture.

They are in the following order, the Emperor's work-room, with fine Empire furniture, the bath-room, the bed-chamber and yellow room, decorated with four pictures by Restout (the Seasons) and two by Oudry (Harvest and Vintage).

NEW APARTMENTS (22-26).

These apartments occupy the right wing of the Villa. They were, after 1704, the apartments of Louis XIV, then those of Louis XV; lastly Louis-Philippe had them restored and furnished (1846) for the reception of the Queen of England, who never came. The furniture has been preserved.

The connoisseur will notice in room 25 two vases of Sevres

CIRCULAR DRAWING-ROOM

porcelain, with bronze stone bases, a vase of Japanese porcelain, called celadon, on a pale green ground, and furniture
covered in Beauvais tapestry; in the bed-chamber (24), two
chests and a console inlaid with ebony and copper, of the
Boulle kind, and a series of old pictures of flowers and mythological subjects.

MUSEUM OF CARRIAGES.

This little museum is situated on the walk connecting the
Great and Small Trianon. It contains state-coaches dating
from the First Empire and the Restoration, and sedan-chairs
and sledges of the 18th century.

The bridles and harness of the horses of the Crown Stables
are in glass cases.

The visitor will notice a *Coronation Car*, built in 1825 for
the coronation-ceremony of Charles X, and restored in 1854,
the ornaments being changed, for the baptism of the son of
Napoleon III. The weight is 15 432 lbs.

The *Baptismal Car*, built in 1821 for the baptism of the
Duke of Bordeaux, was used at the marriage of Napoleon III
and at his son's baptism.

The other carriages date from the time of the First Empire.
The *Topaz* figured in the cortège of Napoleon I's Coronation,
1804. The *Opal* bore the Empress Josephine to the Chateau
of Malmaison, after her divorce.

The only modern vehicle is that which was placed at the
disposition of the Emperor Nicholas II, in Paris and Versailles,
October 1896.

Some very elegant sedan-chairs, of the time of Louis XV
and Louis XVI, complete the exhibition. None of them however
have an authentic history. Neither have the sledges, whose
forms and paintings are so curious; they were used for the
winter pastimes of the court, held in the Versailles Gardens
and on the Grand Canal.

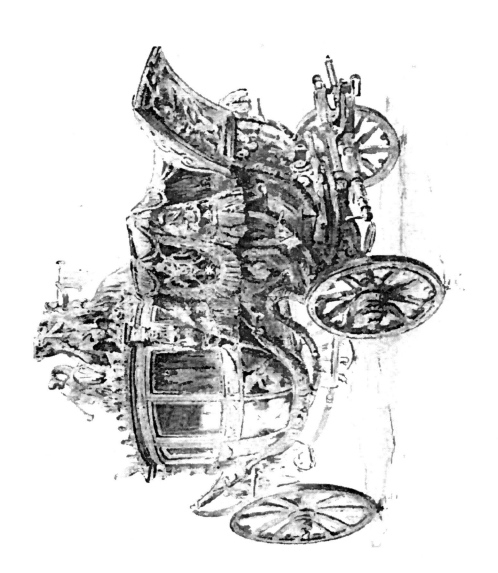

THE LITTLE TRIANON

A grand remembrance of Louis XIV reigns in the Chateau of Versailles where he conceived and executed marvels. At the Grand Trianon, transformed by so many regimes, the one that survives the most is that of Napoleon; at the Petit Trianon there is only one face of which one thinks, that of Marie-Antoinette. The history of the ill-fated Queen, as history so attractive, and so often disfigured by calumny and legend, is here so very realistic. It is this that explains the particular attraction of visitors for this part of the National

8

THE LITTLE TRIANON

HISTORY.

The little villa of Trianon was built by the architect Gabriel towards the close of the reign of Louis XV. This king, being desirous of having in the neighbourhood of Versailles a homely and agreeable resort, decided on the spot where he had placed his green-houses and aviaries. He supped here for the first time in 1708, Here he felt the first symptoms of his last illness, April 27ᵗʰ 1774; he was immediately removed to Versailles, and died thirteen days after.

Louis XVI gave the Little Trianon to Queen Marie-Antoinette, who eagerly took possession and had a delightful English garden made, then called Anglo-Chinese. She often stayed there several weeks with a few friends, and later with her children. She led a country life there, in the simplicity she so loved, away from the pomp and trying etiquette of the Court.

These retreats of the Queen to Trianon occasioned many calumnies against her, from those courtiers she refused to admit. Later, when she had her modest hamlet erected, 1783, people accused her of ruining France with her caprices. Thus the Trianon became fatal to the unfortunate Queen after having given her some of her happiest hours.

On October 5ᵗʰ 1789, Marie-Antoinette was at Trianon when the news of the arrival of the Parisian mob made her leave in haste the dear place she would never see again.

During the First Empire, Princess Pauline Borghèse, favorite sister of Napoleon I, lived in the Little Trianon for some time; under Louis-Philippe, the Duke and Duchess of Orleans inhabited it.

THE LITTLE TRIANON

THE APARTMENTS.

THE STAIRCASE.

Two marvels of French art adorn this staircase : the railing of wrought and gilded iron with the initials M. A. interlaced, and the round lantern of chased and gilded bronze, whose bunch of twelve lights is supported by little seated satyrs.

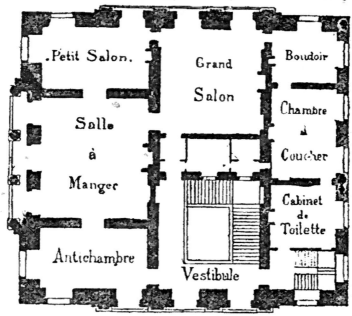

PLAN OF THE APARTMENTS OF THE LITTLE TRIANON

THE ANTEROOM.

The furniture of this and the following rooms is of the time of Louis XVI. There are busts of Louis XVI, by Pajou, and the Emperor Joseph II, brother of Marie-Antoinette, by Boizot. The pictures are by Natoire.

THE STAIRCASE

DINING ROOM.

The decoration of the wainscoting, previous to Marie-Antoinette's time, is taken from the fruits and flowers native to Trianon.

The chased appliqué-work is a true work of art. The stucco table with a geographical chart was designed by Louis XVI for the instruction of the Dauphin.

The lintel is by Pater, master of Watteau. Notice portraits of Louis XVI by Callet, and Marie-Antoinette by M⁽ᵐᵉ⁾ Vigée-Lebrun. The two other pictures were sent by Maria-Theresa to her daughter Marie-Antoinette to recall the scenes of her childhood. That near the window represents the archduchesses, her sisters, playing a Gluck opera at a family performance at Schœnbrunn, on the occasion of the marriage of Joseph II. The other portrays Marie-Antoinette herself dancing with two of her brothers at the same marriage fêtes (1765).

LITTLE HALL.

This was the Queen's billiard-room.

Some fine furniture is shown here. In the centre is an oval table with four mahogany legs, decorated with paintings, bronzes and medallions in biscuit-marble. There is a chandelier with eight lights of the time of Louis XVI.

The jewel-cabinet of Marie-Antoinette is the most sumptuous article made for her. It is of massive mahogany, ornamented with cariatides representing the Four Seasons, rich chased fittings, biscuit medallions, and fine paintings on ivory signed by De Gault, 1787.

The lintel is by Natoire and Lépicié.

LARGE HALL.

The visitor will notice the wainscoting, on which branches of lily are carved, the appliqué-work representing stag-horns

THE QUEEN'S BED ROOM

united by knots of ribbon, the fine furniture covered for the most part with Tours work, the chairs bearing the Queen's monogram. The piano does not belong to the room.

The lintels are by Pater.

Here the Queen entertained her intimate friends, described in detail, as well as the apartments, by M. Nolhac in his book on the *Reign of Marie-Antoinette* (the Chapter on the Trianon).

BOUDOIR.

Some fine wainscoting is composed of the French arms and the monogram of Marie-Antoinette.

The Sèvres bust, copied from Pajou, represents the Queen at the age of eighteen, at the commencement of her reign.

BED-CHAMBER.

The bed, Louis XVI style, is covered with a counterpane of Tours work, embroidered by hand, which belonged to Marie-Antoinette, as did the clock, the inlaid table with the interlaced initials of Louis XVI and Marie-Antoinette, and the chest with chased bronzes by Gouthière.

The pastil is a copy of a precious portrait in oils of Louis XVII, painted by Kucharski in 1792.

GARDENS OF THE LITTLE TRIANON AND HAMLET
OF MARIE-ANTOINETTE.

Leaving the little chateau, the visitor should follow the railing on the left and take the turn opposite. He passes before the *Temple of Love*, a charming erection with a cupola, built on an islet in one of the streams that water the garden.

Continuing, he arrives at *the Hamlet*, a cluster of rustic houses, the principal of which are known by the names of

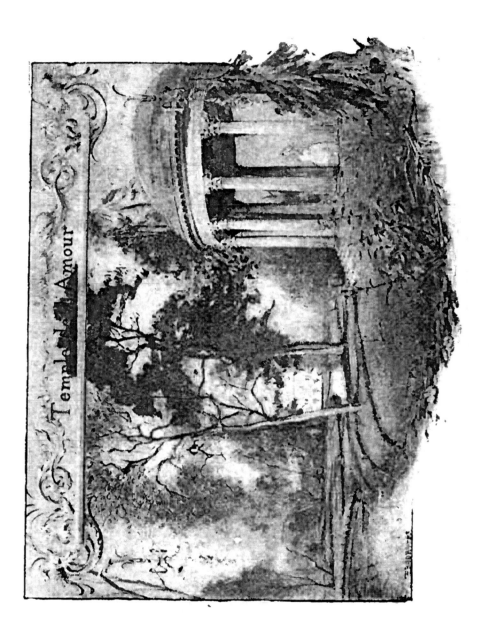

Temple de l'Amour

the Mill (on the left), Billiard-house, the Queen's house, the Hen-house, called also without any reason the Presbytery, the Dairy and Marlborough Tower.

Looking through the Dairy windows, the visitor can see where the Queen without playing in any other way at country life used to prepare cream and butter with her own hands. She used to spend afternoons at the Hamlet with Madame Elisabeth and her friends, all dressed in linen costumes and straw hats, in the most friendly simplicity. Various ridiculous legends have originated about this hamlet, where neither the Queen nor the royal family ever lived or disguised themselves as comic-opera peasants.

The visitor should walk round the little lake and enjoy the views of the Hamlet, noticing at the end the woody swellings on the roots of the Louisiana cypress. These exotic trees were some of those which ornamented the Trianon gardens, and which still form a sufficiently curious collection.

Continuing the walk, visitors will be interested in the Orangery and flower-garden.

Bearing to the left, he comes upon another lake, overtopped by the *Belvedere*, built by Mique, the Queen's architect. The artificial *Rock* is picturesquely designed. Behind the rock are various useful buildings. The principal is the theatre, able to hold 300 at a pinch, where Marie-Antoinette used to perform comedy with the Count of Artois and his private friends.

The garden stretching towards the west of the Chateau is in French style. The pavilion, called the *French Pavilion*, which terminates it and has just been restored, was built under Louis XV, in 1750; it then was used by the King as a summer dining-room.

Behind this pavilion is a modern bridge connecting the Trianon of Marie-Antoinette with that of Louis XIV.

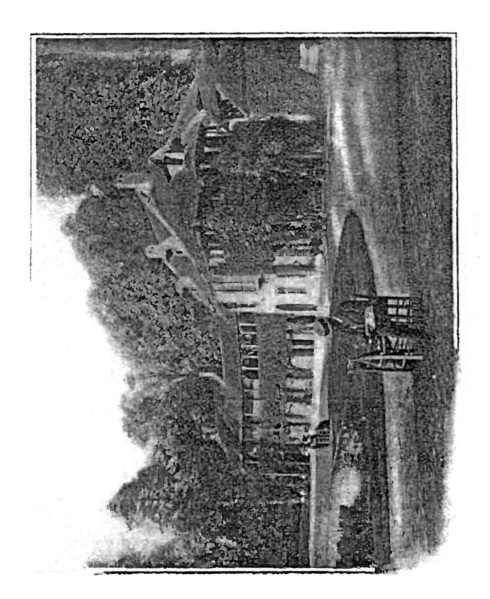

GARDENS OF THE GREAT TRIANON.

These beautiful gardens, which are very extensive and generally deserted, are well worth a visit. The fountains play alternately with those of Versailles.

The most beautiful effect is that of the *Cascade*, also called the *Buffet*, constructed by Mansart, and well restored. It must be viewed from behind the large fountains. The visitor will notice the gilded lead figures (*Neptune* and *Amphitrite*) at the end of a walk, on the right, after passing the corner of the Trianon-in-the-wood.

Turning down the walk on the left of the Buffet, the visitor reaches a large basin called the *Plafond*, also newly restored. Then, returning towards the Palace, he should glance at the terrace overlooking the arm of the Grand Canal, where the Court Flotilla often brought visitors to the beautiful gardens. The view is very extensive.

The only exit from the Great Trianon is a door on the right, reached by passing round the entire building. At the entrance, before the principal gate of the Palace, there are generally carriages waiting to take visitors to Versailles or the stations.

Le Buffet

PARIS

IMPRIMERIE GÉNÉRALE LAHURE

9, rue de Fleurus, 9.

CPSIA information can be obtained at www.ICGtesting.com
Printed in the USA
LVOW09*1417091115

461709LV00003B/4/P